ETHICAL ISSUES

IN THE

PRACTICE OF

ACCOUNTING

Edited by W. Steve Albrecht

*Arthur Andersen Alumni Professor and
Director of the School of Accountancy
and Information Systems
Marriott School of Management
Brigham Young University*

COLLEGE DIVISION South-Western Publishing Co.

Cincinnati Ohio

Sponsoring Editor: Mark R. Hubble
Production Editor: Rebecca Roby
Production House: Custom Publishing Services, Inc.
Cover Design: Graphica
Interior Designer: Lucy Lesiak Design
Marketing Manager: G. M. "Skip" Wenstrup
Sponsoring Representative: Doug Horn

AZ70AA

2 3 4 5 6 7 8 9 D 9 8 7 6 5 4 3 2

Printed in the United States of America

Material from the Professional Code of Ethics, Copyright © 1989, by the American Institute of Certified Public Accountants, is reprinted with permission.

Library of Congress Cataloging-in-Publication Data
Ethical issues in the practice of accounting / edited by W. Steve Albrecht.
        p.   cm.
    Includes bibliographical references.
    ISBN 0-538-81735-6
        1. Accountants—Professional ethics. 2. Auditors—Professional ethics.
3. Accounting—Moral and ethical aspects. 4. Auditing—Moral and ethical
aspects.   I. Albrecht, W. Steve.
HF5657.E857   1991
174'.9657—dc20

Acknowledgment

This book would not have been possible without the help of several key people who made significant contributions. Lois Ritchie's help in administering and planning the conference upon which this book is based was invaluable. Traci Bell who assisted in the preparation of the manuscript provided countless hours of editorial assistance. Catherine Shumway and Cathleen Cornaby, in the 7th floor Word Processing Center, made sure the manuscript for this book was professionally prepared. My research assistant, Alan Clark, provided significant editorial help. Most of all, however, we thank J. David Billeter, a member of the National Advisory Council of the Marriott School of Management who provided significant financial support.

Preface

In all areas of business, ethical dilemmas are encountered frequently. Some of these dilemmas are small and easy to resolve. The majority, however, are complex and an obvious solution is often difficult to determine.

As graduates mature into business professionals, their ethical concerns will change. To cope with such changes, graduates must develop a personal code of ethics which can provide a firm base upon which they can make their decisions.

In the professional accounting field, the focus on ethics has changed significantly. The CPA profession has moved rapidly from a collegial to a competitive environment. With this competition has come increased pressures for recruitment and retention of clients and staff, greater operating efficiency, and better pricing and promotion strategies.

Within industry, concentration on short-term results has placed ethical pressures on accountants and businesses to compromise long-term productivity and gain in order to "maximize the bottom line." Managers at all levels seem to be "seeking the quick buck" instead of considering the long-term profitability of their companies.

Employees of both CPA and industrial firms are caught in the middle of this self-preservation cycle just as are their companies. Allegiance to family and personal lives often conflicts with demands of work and profession. When individuals see employers and associates making compromises in the name of competition and short-term profits or cash flows, they have more difficulty maintaining a strong personal code of ethics.

Ethical challenges that were once addressed through cooperative attitudes now have to be dealt with on a more personal and firm basis. This change of perspective places more importance on the development of a strong personal code of ethics. If one's code is built on sound principles, he or she will not be bothered by changes in practice.

The Basis of This Book

This book on ethics was developed with two purposes in mind.

Purpose 1 — The Development of a Personal Code of Ethics

First, we believe that professionals develop a stronger personal code of ethics when they think about and discuss ethical issues. The process of labeling situations as ethical or unethical is a key ingredient in the "personalization" of ethics. By studying and resolving ethical dilemmas, readers will think through the consequences of their actions in advance and be more likely to develop a firm conviction to act ethically prior to facing compromising situations.

The ability to determine future actions in present circumstances is the goal of each of the cases in this text. As readers experience these situations, they should be encouraged to work out a solution on their own, using the discussion questions provided. This study should allow the reader to develop a personal understanding of their existing values and current ethical strengths.

Following this individual development, group discussions are often exciting and helpful. Group discussions provide the students with the opportunity to consider difficult topics, and to receive pertinent, necessary feedback regarding how their views compare with and are accepted by others.

Often, in ethical situations, no single correct solution exists. Students will come to understand that their personal convictions may be the only foundation upon which they can base their final decisions. If readers are aware of how their personal convictions compare to those of others, they will be more prepared and confident when they are forced to take a position and stand behind it.

Purpose 2 — The Involvement of The Professional Community

The second purpose of the book is to bring together experts in the fields of accounting and ethics who have been actively involved in developing new codes of ethics for business organizations. Through sharing personal experiences, these professionals help us better understand the ethical issues of today's competitive environment.

Table Of Contents

Prologue
Ethical Issues Facing
Accountants

W. STEVE ALBRECHT

Dr. Albrecht received his M.B.A. and doctoral degrees from the University of Wisconsin at Madison. He is presently the Arthur Andersen & Co. Alumni Professor and Director of the School of Accounting and Information System at Brigham Young University. Dr. Albrecht previously taught at Stanford University and at the University of Illinois. He has done extensive research in several areas, including white-collar crime and business fraud.

Introduction

There was once a very wealthy man who loved his money so much that he didn't have many friends. In fact, he had only three friends. First, he had a lawyer friend who helped him structure his transactions to take advantage of other people. Second, he had an accountant friend who helped him count his money. And third, he had a minister friend to whom he went every Sunday to confess the fact that he'd taken advantage of others during the week. Well, when he got old and was about to die, he called his three friends together and said, "I've been wealthy all my life. I can't stand going to the grave poor. I'm going to give you each an envelope with $50,000 in it. I want you to promise me that when I die you'll each go by my casket and each deposit the envelope in the casket." They all promised that they would. A short time later the rich man died. As the three friends passed by the casket, each deposited an envelope. The casket was sealed and the body was buried. Not long after, the minister got a guilty conscience, called the other two and said, "We've got to meet and talk about this." When they met he said, "You know, I thought about the poor members of my congregation. I thought about that money rotting down there in the grave and I just couldn't stand to do it. I only put $25,000 in and I kept $25,000 to help the poor." Then the attorney said, "If you really want to know the truth, he had asked me for free legal advice so often that I felt he owed it to me, so I kept $25,000 and only put $25,000 in." Finally, the accountant said, "You know, I can't believe you would do it. I can't believe you both would be unethical. I want you to know that in my envelope was a check for the full $50,000."

Focusing on the difficulty of ethics, do you think the accountant was unethical or was he merely smart? And who, of the three, was the most unethical? These are difficult issues. This book is primarily designed for accounting issues, but if you're not an accountant, if you happen to be in a general business of some sort, you will also benefit because the ethical issues that are discussed are relevant to all areas of business.

The Erosion of Ethics

We are all familiar with the eroding ethics around us. All you have to do is read the newspaper. We read about college coaches and currently one athletic conference that has five of its ten schools on probation for recruiting violations. We hear of congressmen with ethical problems and investment bankers, such as Mike Milken and Ivan Boesky. And we hear about ministers. First we have an unethical minister and then we have another accusing him of being unethical. Then, we find that the accuser is unethical too. We have all kinds of ethical problems in all walks of society, including business leaders. A recent study has been done by two professors, one from Florida and one from Minnesota. They surveyed 7,000 retail employees — first in 1962 and then again in 1986. Their results were that in 1962, 12 percent of the people were inclined to be dishonest in the corporate environment. When they repeated the study in 1986, 30 percent were inclined to be dishonest. Unethical attitudes increased from 12 to 30 percent.

Ethics Among Accountants

I recently completed a study of my own with a Fortune 500 company where we looked at 2,200 employees. Six percent said they had done something dishonest which cost their firm over $100. Thirty-three percent said they had seen somebody else do something dishonest. We see all these dishonest, unethical actions throughout society, but what about accountants? Are accountants dishonest or unethical? The AICPA recently sponsored a survey that was conducted by Lou Harris and Associates. Among other things, they had the respondents rate accountants on the following six pivotal attributes: honesty, competence, reliability, objectivity, concern for public interest, and creativity. Notably, accountants ranked highest in the area of honesty. In fact, accountants are perceived as being even more honest than they are competent and reliable. On the other hand, they ranked lowest in the area of creativity, although that may just be a perception. In any event, one thing is certain — accountants have a lot of influence.

Not too long ago I was talking with two friends, one a medical doctor and the other a stockbroker. During the course of our conversation the stockbroker spoke up and said, "How come accountants have so much power?" I asked, "What do you mean?" He replied, "Well, I have a client that I've worked with for 12 years. All of a sudden his accountant tells him, 'You've got to find a new broker because I can't read this statement.' Without further argument, my client immediately set out to find a new broker. Now because we, as accountants have so much influence, we want to make sure that our influence is felt in ethical ways.

We do have examples of unethical accountants. In fact, a following chapter of this book is authored by a CPA who worked in public accounting, became controller of a bank, and embezzled over $100,000 from that bank. We're all familiar with a CPA by the name of Gomez who took bribes of approximately $150,000 under the table to hide a major fraud of a client called ESM. Recently, the SEC sanctioned a CPA because he gave a clean opinion on a client and didn't look at any records. Instead, he accepted personal representations of management. In fact, the company didn't have any records except a check register.

Often I'm asked why there is so much unethical behavior and fraud. I really don't know whether it's increasing in amount or we're just hearing about it more. But we're certainly hearing about it more.

Fraud is just one type of unethical behavior, but it is one that illustrates some basic principles. We know that people commit fraud because of a combination of three factors: pressure, opportunity, and rationalization. First, a financial pressure or some kind of nonshareable need exists in their life. This pressure, not necessarily financial, is combined with a perceived opportunity to get away with an act, and then some way to rationalize it as being acceptable. Let me give an example and then I'll discuss ethics in general. I once talked to a young woman, 18 years old, who grew up in a strong Catholic family. This family was very religious and disdained premarital sex. They had taught their children that premarital sex was wrong. Unfortunately, this girl got pregnant. She avoided telling her family for fear of disappointing her mom and dad. Consequently, she decided to get an abortion, but didn't have any money to fund it. So, she took advantage of an opportunity where she worked to steal $300 to fund the abortion. Afterwards, she stole again, and before she was caught her fraud totalled $86,000. It was a financial pressure, the need to fund the abortion, that started the crime. From there it snowballed. The pressure was the financial need, she had an opportunity, and her initial rationalization was that, "I am going to pay the money back. I'm just temporarily borrowing it to fund this abortion." Like many others, she got caught up in the situation and found that it wasn't as easy to pay back as she thought. I suspect that some of the unethical behavior we have in accounting and in business is because we have pressures, opportunities and rationalizations.

Let me identify a couple of pressures on accountants — time pressures, reduced fees, client pressures for clean opinions, client pressures to pay less taxes, increased competition for clients, and on and on. What about opportunities? Accountants work in an environment where it is very difficult to judge the quality of their work. In an audit, for example, the only tangible output is contained in two or three paragraphs. It is difficult to judge the quality of the work that went into that opinion. Another opportunity lies in the complicated tax laws. It's very easy to cheat in the area of taxes. Finally, another opportunity is the low frequency of reviews by outsiders. And, what about rationalizations? It's easy to rationalize in many areas of accounting. We have the notion that everybody's cheating a little bit on their taxes. That's rationalization. When somebody like a president of the United States says the tax system is a national disaster, some of us use that as rationalization to pay as little as possible, anyway we can get away with it. There is less honesty training in society and many cases of dishonesty which are highly publicized. All of these cases lead to rationalizations.

Those who study moral development tell us that people develop strong codes of ethics when two things happen: first, you have to label situations as honest or dishonest, and second, you have to model honesty. In other words, be a good example! We're seeing much more of this today in corporate America. We're seeing companies labeling honesty and dishonesty with codes of conduct and with strong prosecution policies. There is evidence of more labeling of honesty and ethics than ever before.

Very little research has been done in the area of ethics in accounting. The ethical issues facing accountants are not well articulated and specific. For example, is sex discrimination an ethical issue? I think it might be. How about copying software? How about doing work that we're not qualified for? How about producing misleading advertising claims saying that we can perform in areas that we can't? What about giving faulty investment advice or helping clients evade taxes? How about not keeping up professionally? How about caving into client pressures or showing favoritism in promotion? How about promoting certain things as healthy in your environment?

Outline of the Book

There are many ethical issues related to accounting. This book deals with several of the most difficult. Chapter 1 discusses the need for Ethics education for accountants and business managers. It's author, Michael S. Josephson is President of The Joseph and Edna Josephson

Institute for the Advancement of Ethics and is one of the most widely quoted spokesmen on Ethics in America today. Chapters 2 and 3 deal with broad ethical issues in the practice of accounting. Authors of these chapters are Robert J. Sack, previously chief accountant of the SEC's Enforcement Division and William Hall, retired Arthur Andersen & Co. partner and consultant to Andersen's Business Ethics Program. Chapter 4 discusses the new AICPA's Code of Ethics for Accountants. It's author, George Anderson, is a past chairman of the AICPA and chairman of the committee that drafted the new Ethics Code.

Chapters 5 through 12 discuss ethical issues in the four major types of accounting work: audit, tax, systems and management consulting, and management accounting. For each of these topics, there is a chapter identifying the major types of ethical dilemmas accountants face. Authors of these four chapters are L. Glenn Perry (audit), partner with KPMG Peat Marwick, and past chief accountant of the SEC's Division of Enforcement; James B. Dox (tax), partner in charge of tax for the Los Angeles Office of Ernst and Young; J. Owen Cherrington (systems and management consulting), Professor of Accounting at Brigham Young University and frequent writer and consultant on Ethics Issues in Management Consulting; and Daniel R. Coulson (management accounting), accounting director for Ford Motor Company's Finance Staff. To give practical applications to ethical dilemmas accountants face in these four areas, each of these topical chapters is followed by a chapter which includes a relevant ethics case and question and answer discussion of the case by experts in the area. These case discussion chapters are authored by four Brigham Young University Accounting professors: Larry Deppe (audit), David N. Stewart (tax), Eric Denna (systems and management consulting), and Richard McDermott (management accounting).

Chapters 13 through 15 deal with one of the most problematical issues in accounting today — ethical issues facing young professional accountants. Chapter 13 is authored by Loree Dunn Hagen, a Price Waterhouse manager who has worked as an accountant for five years. Chapter 15 includes a practical case on ethical issues facing young professional accountants and a question and answer discussion of the case by professional accountants. It is authored by James D. Stice, an accounting faculty member at Brigham Young University. Chapter 16 includes a confession and discussion by a former CPA, McKinley L. Tabor, who compromised his Code of Ethics and embezzled from the bank where he worked as tax controller. The chapter includes both an analysis of his fraud and questions to him by professional accountants. The book concludes with a brief postlogue by a Brigham Young University Professor who read these chapters and offered his analysis of what ethical lessons can be gleaned from these pages. At the back of the book is a collection of interesting quotes on ethics and a bibliography which we hope will be valuable as you think about and consider ethical issues in accounting.

Our hope is that this book will serve as a means for having you think about ethical issues. We believe that by doing so, your personal commitment to strong ethics will be reinforced. The process of thinking about tough ethical issues is a key ingredient in one's "personalization" of ethics.

1
The Need for Ethics Education in Accounting___

DR. MICHAEL S. JOSEPHSON

Dr. Josephson is a graduate of both UCLA and UCLA Law School. He is the founding president of the Joseph and Edna Josephson Institute for the Advancement of Ethics, as well as the founder of a legal educational company. He is author of numerous articles and books which include extensive information on values and ethics.

Introduction ___

Virtually every program focusing on ethics begins with the explicit, if not implicit question, "Are things really any worse?" Are we just reading more about ethical problems or are there really more ethical problems now than ever before? As with most issues, there's a spectrum of responses to these questions. On the one end of the spectrum, there are the doomsayers and alarmists who genuinely seem to believe we're in a state of moral crisis. In fact, things have never been worse than they are now and they're getting worse all the time. On the other side are the casual apologists who will say, "No, things aren't so bad; in fact, they've never been better." Not surprisingly, both can cite substantial evidence to support their position.

The Alarmists' View: Corruption in Business Ethics ___

For example, the alarmist, or the doomsayers will say, "Just look at what's going on in our society, particularly, the securities industry. First, there was E.F. Hutton in check kiting. Then the insider trading situation arose. We are familiar with 'Greed is Good' Boesky and now the half a billion dollar man, Mike Milken. This whole process of insider trading seems to be corrupt from within some of our major institutions." But that's not all. Consider defense procurement. Major companies such as Teledyne, Northrup, and Unysis, are all involved in various ways. General Dynamics has also appeared with what

___
Reprinted by permission of Dr. Michael S. Josephson.

seems to be an unabated stream of cheating and overcharging. Further, what about the banking industry? Not long ago money laundering schemes were evidenced by some of the nation's largest banks which were involved in evading—and in some cases—clearly breaking currency laws to launder money for crooks. Now there is the savings and loan problem which can be explained on all kinds of bases, but there's no question that there was rampant mismanagement and extreme cases of fraud. Some people even think the accountants had some complicity in that. Perhaps the accountants had some real responsibilities to either uncover and report the problem or do something more affirmative than they did. Thus, in looking at all of these industries one might conclude that, "Everywhere we look there is corruption."

There was the Ford Pinto case some years ago in which they tried to conceal their rear gas tank scandal. There was the asbestos scandal. And most recently, A.J. Robbins had the problem with the Dalcon Shield. Recently there was Beech Nut, makers of baby food, selling apple-less apple juice. Juice that had no apples at all causing the president of that very large and prestigious company to go to jail, or at least be sentenced to jail. (His sentence was later reversed on a technicality on appeal.) There is number one Hertz Rent-A-Car admitting to rampant fraud and forgery in an insurance scam against their own customers. And then, there was the issue of Exxon. It's not clear whether Exxon really did anything wrong, but it certainly added to the blemish that exists on the business reputation in general.

Ethical Problems in Accounting

More and more the old joke is told, where the firm asks its accountant how much is 2+2. The accountant replies, "How much do you want it to be?" More and more it is implied that accountants are giving in to the bottom line pressures just like everybody else. In many cases they see themselves as employees or agents of their clients. On the one hand, such an attitude is quite understandable and predictable. On the other hand, it seems to be undermining the notions of independence and objectivity that have so long marked the profession of advocacy. Today, major accounting firms offer a cafeteria of financial services. Many accounting firms will offer virtually anything a client wants, without necessarily thinking of how it affects the culture of their organization. As more and more nonaccountants become involved in major decision making situations, they might not, in fact, be imbued with all of the commitments and understanding of what public accounting ought to be. Currently, the problem exists with commissions and contingency fees and the FTC's opposition of a ban on such fees. Interestingly, although accountants originally opposed this idea, more and more often are saying, "Maybe it won't be such a bad thing after all." Although this view isn't necessarily wrong, the reason things are happening aren't always right either. Much of what is happening is due to pressures rather than because of intelligent decisions based on desired behavior.

With the alarmists' view, there truly is evidence indicating that things are getting worse. The evidence is rampant and pervasive throughout business, including accounting.

The Apologists' View: Business Ethics Are Sound _____

In contrast, the apologists argue that these examples are all taken out of context. Recently, I participated in a program for U.S. military generals and one of the first things I was told was, "You hear all about the $600 toilet seats and the cheating that goes on. We don't make excuses for that. We shouldn't have it. But do you know that we make 30 million acquisitions a year and out of those 30 million only 10-20 mistakes are reported? Who has a better batting average than we?" As a result, you see people trying to apply another kind of perspective. They say, "These are just aberrations from the normal course of business, which in fact has higher ethics than ever before. Admittedly, there is good evidence for that. If you look over the last 20-25 years, the movement, in terms of corporate responsibility, has been only in one direction. It has been toward much more responsibility. Corporations are accepting responsibilities with respect to the environment, product safety and healthier working conditions, and also less discrimination. The direction has been good in trying to repress or suppress sexual harassment. Plant closing and layoffs are usually done more humanely than before. Even leveraged buyouts (LBOs) are argued not simply to be a corrupt decision which encourages greed, but as a way to help make America more efficient and competitive."

The Neutral View: The Actual Position of Business _____

Who's right? Are things getting worse, or are they actually getting better? My honest assessment is that it's a little of each. On one level, institutionally, things are getting better. Not only in business, but in politics and journalism as well. Institutional and professional ethics have shown vast improvement. We are now criticizing behavior in politics and journalism and other fields that were not even thought to be worthy of criticism 10, 15, or 20 years ago. This, because we are ratcheting up our expectations. The problem is that most of the expectations which have created a greater sense of ethical sensitivity and diminished conflicts of interest, have been the result of regulation. Unfortunately, they have not been the result of voluntary determinations by any of the bodies that are affected. Although this regulation has vastly improved consumer protection, the result makes it even more evident that people can substitute legal requirements, rules and standards for moral autonomy and moral judgment. That is a real danger. We are becoming such a legalistic society that we don't make determinations for ourselves of what is right or wrong.

While institutionally we may in fact be becoming more responsible and more moral, it can be proven that in every profession, individually, we may be becoming much less responsible. Our moral muscles are atrophying due to so much regulation and so many rules. People simply ask the question now, "Is it legal?" The assumption seems to be, if it's permissible, it's proper. The assumption seems to be: if you have a right to do something, it is right to do it. Yet, when we reflect on the meaning of ethics we know this has never been nor can ever be the true standard of ethical behavior. Legal standards will and always have to be, by their nature, consensus minimal standards of impropriety. They are consensus minimal standards of impropriety because we say anybody who falls below this line is a crook, and we'll punish them. However, just because you escape the label of a crook and escape punishment does not necessarily imply that you have done the right thing.

It is clear that an ethical person often does more than they have to do. Alternatively, an unethical person often does less than they're allowed to do. This is an exceptionally difficult situation in many of the professions, such as law and accounting, and in some cases business, which require one to act in a representational capacity. The question arises, "Do I have a right to require more than the law requires, or to do less than the law allows in a representational capacity?" This is one of the great ethical challenges of the professions. Where, if anywhere, is there room for individual moral autonomy? Is there a balance between becoming some moral, self-righteous imperialist who imposes your "high standards" on another at their cost, or, on the other hand, becoming so ethically flexible and loose that you can adapt to the standards, requirements and self-serving demands of everyone?

Ethical Responsibility

Ultimately, the point is that although much evidence indicates that the ethical situation is getting better, there's also much evidence that it is getting worse. In any event, however, you don't have to be sick to get better. There's absolutely no question that we, in the professions could make a significant social contribution if we took our responsibilities affecting the culture more seriously and more directly.

First, we must be very cautious about becoming increasingly more cynical. One of the effects of the tremendous amount of press coverage on all these terrible events is that soon, like anything else, you get calloused. The accountant is no different than the doctor who gets calloused to deaths and the lawyer who gets calloused to having people sent to jail. Because you get calloused, soon each crime is just another scandal. You begin to expect it. There is a serious down side to this cynicism. It changes our expectations and ultimately our aspirations because when we get so cynical that we don't expect more out of others and soon we don't expect much more out of ourselves. This is a psychological reality that professionals need to guard against. Hopefully, accountants will preserve and fight to keep their righteous indignation. When someone within society, and especially within our profession, violates fundamental principles of goodness, decency, honesty, and integrity, we must vehemently object. There are many excuses: "I'd like to be ethical, but...my competitors won't let me, the state of the economy won't let me, my individual boss won't let me, or our shareholders won't let us."

There are a million ways to pass off the responsibility. Among the best of the 'pass-the-buck people' are accountants. You ask an accountant a tough ethical question and he'll answer, "That is the senior partner's responsibility." Accountants can usually sidestep the issue and they find relief in knowing that. Someone else always has to make tough decisions. Yet, the fact of the matter is, one chooses by not making the choice. Personal accountability requires that we be accountable for what we produce. Remember what Lily Tomlin said, "The problem with the rat race is that even if you win, you're still a rat." We can't lose sight of that by getting so very cynical.

The danger of cynicism is that the naive American idealism which has long been associated with this country will totally deteriorate and we'll be cynical just like the Europeans. They can't understand why most of our scandals even make the news. If we lose that idealism, we start to buy into a no-holds barred, everybody for himself, look out for number one, philosophy. This is illustrated by a little story which has great impact. An MBA goes out on a camping trip with his friend and they look up and they see a cougar. It's only about 20 yards away. All of a sudden the MBA starts to take off his backpack, and the friend asks, "What are you going to do?" The MBA replied, "Well, I'm going to run for it." "But you can't outrun a cougar," answered the friend, and the MBA says, "But I don't have to outrun the cougar, I just have to outrun you." If that seems a little dramatic, reconsider some of the examples you may have known or may have seen where, in fact, survival of the fittest is the operational standard. Such survival tactics cut against what the fundamentals of ethics really are.

The Importance of the Accounting Group

Why is the accounting group so important? Because it is composed of a group of leaders. There are people who look up to you over whom you have some authority and responsibility. In addition, some are teachers who have a direct responsibility to provide the fundamental education for the people that are going to enter the accounting field and business in general. Further, those who are already in the professions have a responsibility both to the firms and to society as a whole to check on the education of these people, to reeducate them if necessary, and to establish the kind of standards that are consistent with the image the organization wants to convey. Passing it off to somebody else is not good enough. Of all the professions, accounting is the most natural to be considered the appropriate heart and conscience of business. Accounting has always had an odd relationship with business. On the one hand you are an advisor and advocate and on the other hand you are a kind of a censor, sometimes even a policeman. You often must say, "Beyond this point you may not go." Interestingly, this has been one of the critical attributes of accountancy that has allowed accountants to be the most respected profession in the United States for years. Most recent polls reconfirm that most people believe accountants are the most honest of all the professionals. You are perceived to have the greatest amount of integrity. Society expects that integrity to manifest itself when there are pressures and when people want to sacrifice and compromise principles. Sometimes the accountant is referred to as the abominable no-man. Some people refer to the controller as the sales prevention department. But the fact of the matter is, when the accountants do their jobs well, they are providing a counter force which goes against the steady stream of self-interest. You are, in fact, the natural conscience of a company.

It is so much harder today to be that conscience when you are more and more co-opted by the companies that you serve. You're coopted simply because of the amount of money involved and the importance the client provides to your own firm. And, in many cases, you get coopted on a personal basis. You like these people; you care about them; you are involved in their business; and you want them to succeed. All these forces inherently and naturally cut against your ability to provide objective, stern, rigorous judgment. Those who teach the young associates in your firms must point out the pressures that they will, in fact, face. These pressures are unpredictable. It is absolutely mandatory that young professionals be told that there will be times when there are reasons, from self interests to compassion, which could lead them to compromise what they believe or know to be right. Prepare yourself and develop strategies to anticipate such situations and deal with them effectively.

It is disturbing to hear more and more accountants adopt the language of their more competitive MBA compatriots. Today, you hear accountants saying, "We've got mortgages, too; we've got to send our kids to college; we're in an incredibly competitive environment now; we're not only in the accounting business, we're in financial services and every other kind of business." The implication from these statments can be illustrated by a scene from a play by Arthur Miller, called "All My Sons." In the play the son discovers that his father really had clay feet; he'd done some things in business that really weren't very acceptable. The father had always been a hero to the son. The father says, knowing that losing the esteem of his son is probably one of the greatest losses he can have, "Son, I'm sorry. But, really, I'm no worse than anyone else." The son replied, "Dad, I know. But I thought you were better." This is the challenge of ethics— to be better. The challenge of ethics is not to be "no worse than anybody else," not to justify and forgive yourself for the compromises you made, but to recognize that some people think you're better. You went into this profession thinking you were better. And you can be better. But it's hard. Being better is hard.

The Power of Rationalization

There is a magazine entitled, *Ethics, Easier Said Than Done*. I stress this title because I think it's a mistake to be too pious or too glib or too sanctimonious about "Let's all be ethical." There are very good and compelling reasons why fundamentally decent people do indecent or improper things. And many of them, still to this day, don't think they are indecent or improper because they filter things through their rationalizations.

People should be made aware of this in order to help them fortify their consciences against the things that will tend to make inroads. The first step is to recognize that the natural rationalization process that occurs when our own self interest is at stake creates the need for an outside voice. Whenever we have a large personal stake in a decision that has significant ethical implications, we need an outside voice because we are just too smart today. We're too clever and we can rationalize it. Consider this example. A group of editors in a major midwest newspaper were faced with an ethical dilemma. They had discovered the whereabouts of a kidnap victim before the police did. But, they concluded that the victim was safe because of the odd situation. Besides, it was going to be a terrific story. Well, they had to decide whether they should tell the police or whether they were going to wait until morning to get a picture and story.

Journalists, almost invariably, labor hard over ethical issues. Usually, they end up concluding whatever is expedient. So after much debate and soul searching lasting late into the night, they decided the person was safe—that they wouldn't call the police. Finally, one of the editors realized what time it was and felt the need to call home to his wife. Knowing about the problem she asked,

"What did you decide?" He told her their decision and began to explain. She didn't even let him finish. She said, "You what!? How dare you take that upon yourself." In two minutes she destroyed every argument with her simple stab of conscience. Needless to say, the decision was reversed.

The point is that so many of the tough decisions we have to make are decisions where we are, in fact, major stakeholders. You'll want to rationalize and say, 'it's not my interest at stake, it's the clients.' But, it is your interest that's at stake. It's your prestige, your clientele, and your fee. Whether you admit you're right or wrong, you may be putting your neck on the line. When self-interest is involved, which is almost always, you need to have the benefit of an outside voice. It would be nice if that outside voice could be provided from within your own firm. However, often that is not possible because your colleagues themselves are tied up with the same interest. You can, however, at least help make people aware of the seductive temptation of self interest, not because they are any more selfish than anyone else, but precisely because they are just as vulnerable as anybody else to self-serving rationalizations.

The second point to consider is how easily different professions, in the course of their work, start to translate their job into a sort of gamesmanship theory where winning becomes a moral imperative. This occurs in every profession. With politicians, what do you think the moral imperative is? It's getting re-elected. Why is it a moral imperative? It's because "I can't do all the good I'm going to do unless I have the power."

What is the moral imperative for the journalist? It's getting the story. The public has a right to know, it's in the First Amendment. Clothe yourself in some self-righteous argument and you can do almost anything. Because getting the story is critical, sacrificing a nuance here and there in order to achieve the goal, is ethically justified. In other words, the end justifies the means.

What is the moral imperative in business? In the general sense, it is to make a profit—to succeed. However, in reality it isn't really to make a profit, is it? It certainly is not sufficient for the major public companies to make a profit. It's not even sufficient to make a reasonable profit. It is required to make the maximum profit every 90 days. In fact, meeting the business plan becomes the moral imperative. Staving off the people on Wall Street; including the stockbrokers and the investment analysts, and offsetting what they will say is the moral imperative. Along with this imperative comes the excuse, "I'm really not doing this for myself; I'm doing it for others. Look at all the jobs I'm saving, not the least of which is my own." But the fact of the matter is that, while these things are important, the lawyer's moral imperative is to win for his client and the accountant's is to be a good representative for his client. Unfortunately, sometimes accountants think they are like lawyers. Other times they think they are auditors who are acting independently. They flip-flop.

If you believe you have a moral obligation to win, you will do whatever it takes to win. Politicians have said, "I'd like to be honest, but they won't let me." Who are "they?" The electorate? "If I really told them that we have to raise taxes, they won't elect me." Admittedly, there's some evidence to support their concern. Because the electorate is acting without principal or conscience, the elected official has to act without principal or conscience. Finally, he says, "I'll be as honest as I can be." And that means he will be as dishonest as he has to be.

I met one politician during an ethics program who said, "There's sure is a lot of lying up here. I hardly ever lie." I responded, "Do you hardly ever take bribes?" In other words, what is "hardly ever." One of the problems is, we judge ourselves by our good intentions. We judge ourselves through our own glasses of how good we intend to be, how good we want to be, including all the excuses. We've already filtered out our weaknesses. In contrast, how do we judge others? We don't judge others by their good intentions. We judge them by their actions. We also judge others on how they go about achieving their good intentions. Sometimes a good intention can be destroyed because the method of achieving it is unacceptable. Ultimately, though, the end justifies the means' philosophy emerges. Attitudes surface such as: judge me by my good intentions, judge me as a whole, judge me on the average. In honesty surveys most people say, "I'm basically honest." What does "basically honest" mean? It means, if it doesn't cost too much I'll be honest. If you say you're basically honest it means you're willing to be dishonest. And when do you think you're willing to be dishonest—when it's important. That is precisely the times you need to be honest. That is the terrific challenge!

The Relationship Between Business and Ethics

What I hope to teach you people is that ethics has nothing to do with business. It is a separate, independent mode of evaluation that applies to all conduct. Ethics is like your skin—it goes with you everywhere. This moral point of view asks you to judge your conduct in terms of right and wrong, decency, honesty, goodness, and honor. A common misconception is that "good ethics is good business." Deep down inside we know that's not true even though you might want to believe it. Too many examples cite situations where good ethics hasn't been good business for individuals. It is true that good ethics is good business in the long run for industries and organizations. But, how many people are interested in the long run? After all, "Who's going to care if I don't meet my business plan this quarter, when there's a good chance I won't be here? Tell me why it's good business for me?" Granted, it's good for your integrity and your self-image, but there are all kinds of middle managers who never want to hire another middle manager who won't get on the program. `Whose side are you on' is the implicit question that is asked.

I suggest that the fields of battle are strewn with bodies of people who were ethical, who stood up for their ethics and because of it they paid a price. Just like people who died in the war, they are good people. Goodness does not guarantee winning. And unless we can teach and emphasize this point, people will look for the angle. Naturally, they are always seeking a win-win situation. If they can't see the win on both sides, the philosophy of good ethics as good business is quickly translated in the mind to: good business therefore must be good ethics.

Consider, for example, a company which has a line of credit. For the third quarter in a row they failed to meet projections. Finally their bank said, "If you don't meet your projections this quarter, we must call the loan." As a result, the company will be insolvent. This was their last hope for loans. The CFO is approached, "What can you do for us? Aren't there some invoices we can move around? Can we declare income a little earlier? Can we understate bad debts? Overstate assets? We need help." How can being ethical be good business if the CFO, along with others, will lose his job? Granted, conscience is important. One must be able to live with himself. But it is surprising to note how many people can sleep with the things they've done. How shockingly easy it is to delude the conscience and convince yourself that what you did is alright. Hitler could sleep.

I met one executive who was absolutely sure he knew what was right. When asked, "How do you know you're doing the right thing," he replied, "Because I did it and I wouldn't have done it unless it was right." That lack of self-examination, that assumption that you're instincts are highly refined, that your moral balance is undisturbed by the outside forces is really preposterous and pretentious because we are all human beings. The issue is to recognize and teach people that there are in fact reasons why it is hard to be ethical.

Why We Should Be Ethical

The reason to be ethical is simply because it is right. Everyone who gives an enlightened self-interest argument compromises the ideal that ethics is right, based on the theory that virtue is its own reward, and that's just how we're supposed to behave if we're good people. What's the point of being a good person if there's no pay off? I suggest that while we do have capacity as humans to be awfully venal and to do awfully bad deeds, we all have the capacity to do awfully noble acts and to have natural compassion.

If it seems we're getting hardened in this society, think back to individuals' reactions when the Challenger explosion occurred and the astronauts died. Most of us didn't even know who they were. But, I'll bet most people cried or came close to crying. Remember the feelings surrounding little Jessica McClure when she was discovered in that pipe in Texas. No one knew her, but there was a natural caring and compassion.

Even when working with the non-profit community for both foundations and for non-profit organizations, I am startled and disturbed by the ease with which they have moved into the business jargon of saying, "Go tell contributors what's in it for them." Sometimes they persuade beyond any realism. They think the only way to get business people to contribute is to convince them that they're making an investment. I have nothing against that kind of giving. Just don't call it philanthropy—it's marketing. It's alright to believe that donations are good marketing investments; but don't squeeze out the possibility of genuine caring and genuine giving. Don't squeeze out the possibility that there are people who say, "I don't care what's in it for me, I want to help." Unfortunately, what's happening is we all have bought into the idea that it's irrational to act any other way except on self interest. We're even beginning to lose the rhetoric, "Ask not what your country can do for you, but what you can do for your country." This statement made a lot of difference in my life and it is one of the reasons I am actively involved in promoting ethics. When I sold my own company, I decided to invest a significant part of the money. However, I'm no goody two shoes who doesn't know about the practical world. As a matter of fact, I had a business, started it from scratch, and sold it for $10 million. I put $1 million into the Institute that I named after my parents; not to be noble but because that's what I wanted to do. Call it selfish. I don't call it noble. But the fact of the matter is people can give, people can care. I work now for the Institute at no salary whatsoever because I'm fortunate enough, even after taxes, to invest enough to live on. Some say, "Oh, sure, it's easy for you. You have the luxury of being ethical." However, that's just another one of the fallacies: ethics is a luxury. "I'll get to it next year when I'm making enough." When do you think you're going to make enough? You never make enough!

The Importance of Enduring Ethical Values

A survey done some time ago asked people how much more money they really needed to make, beyond what they are making now, to be reasonably comfortable. No matter what people were making, everything from $20,000 a year to $200,000 a year, the average answer was that a 10-15 percent increase in income signified comfortable living standards. Regardless of the individual, the number was always within their shooting distance, just ratcheted up to fit their individual needs. In other words, they all just ratcheted up their demands.

That's a bad race to be in. It's a no-win race. We've got to try to introduce this idea to the young people now. They won't fully understand it. But a seed will be planted and it will grow and take hold when they begin to acquire material items. For instance, when they get their first BMW and it will be a thrill for about a week.

I remember vividly doing my very first business plan. As a law professor I started a business, a bar review course preparing people for bar examinations. A five-year business plan was required because I was getting a loan. Projecting out five years seemed preposterous to me. I had no idea what I was doing. I said, "This is ridiculous! How could I possibly know? What will happen five years from now?" But the bank insisted, so I proceeded to guess. I remember guessing that by the third year we ought to gross $1 million. I never believed it because I couldn't imagine anything I was involved in grossing a million dollars. But it seemed logical and I really wasn't making it up. These were honest projections, yet I didn't believe it. However, in the third year we did gross a million dollars and the sense of achievement I had was enormous, but incredibly short-lived. Then my thoughts turned toward making $2 million.

I remember the first year I ever took home $100,000. I never thought it would be possible because I was in academia. I chose against the business world although I did get into business on the side. In 1977, I took home $100,000 and truly felt rich! It lasted a month and soon I had to deal with my income. How should it be invested? Am I going to get a bigger house? Am I going to get a bigger car? Soon, my money became a burden.

In contrast, I am reminded of another experience which happened about seven years into my teaching career. I was at a conference for the Association of American Law Schools when a man approached me and said, "I just wanted to thank you. I'm sure you don't remember me but you were at Hamlin Law School about four years ago and you sat down and talked to me. I was having real troubles deciding whether I wanted to stay in law school. I doubted that I could pass the bar exam. You talked to me and helped me enormously. In my opinion, you changed my life. I've just been appointed the first Mexican-American Dean in the United States."

To this moment it gives me a chill to recall that story. And when I compare that sense of achievement, that sense of self-esteem and worth to the feelings I get when I look instead at how much I've made, what I've accumulated, and the art in my home there's no comparisons. In fact, I'm embarrassed to admit how infrequently I look at my wonderful art, let alone enjoy it! There is inherent emptiness in such accumulations. That isn't to say that poverty is good. Rich is better than poor. But the fact of the matter is we must focus on what endures.

According to a wise man, nobody ever said on their death bed, "I wish I spent more time at the office." Because at that point, what matters is the enduring values, including what you have done, what you have achieved. The things that you're struggling for right now, the three top problems you think you have right now are probably inconsequential in the long term. The real problems are how you relate to your children, how you relate to your spouse, what are you doing for your country and your neighbors. Those are the things that last. The rest, the quarterly plan, whether or not you get this client, whether or not you get an A in school, whether you get this job, is all going to disappear into incredible insignificance at some point. That doesn't mean you don't strive and don't compete to do the best. It means you must have perspective. We must teach people to step back and see the big picture.

A Definition of Ethics

Once people are convinced that ethics is important and that ethics is good, we move to the problem of defining what ethics means. One problem in defining ethics is that we tend to think of ethics as being in three main areas: sex, politics, and religion. In each of those three areas there is incredible diversity. People have very different attitudes as to what is or is not acceptable sexually. As for religion, people firmly believe that they have the way. But we also know that the world is divided into so many different religions and so many beliefs that clearly, for one person to be right the others have to be wrong. As a result we adopt this benign tolerance, "I'm pretty sure I'm right but I forgive them for being wrong." With politics, we translate some of our deeply held beliefs into moral imperatives. Communism is a vicious plot against humanity. Socialism is also, as are some individual politicians. The problem is, when we think about ethics we tend to think about morality—meaning, attitudes about sex, religion, and politics. However, if we have learned anything in this country, it is that our country is diverse and has gotten its strength from the tolerance of that diversity. The mistake we make is in thinking of ethics as a package with no enduring, universal values. In fact, I suggest to you the opposite.

The Components of an Ethical Person _____

Think of the one or two most ethical people you know—somebody you really respect as being ethical. How many people do you think would list you when asked that question? Is that important to you? Would you like to be on the list when people associated with you are asked, "Who is the most ethical person you know?" Statistically, you are probably not on that list. In fact, you're probably not on anyone's list at all. Why? What are you not doing that you ought to be doing? Most people would like to be on the list suggesting the idea of ethical commitment. People want to be ethical, which is why they rationalize so hard and work so hard to justify what they do. Think again of this person that you regard as ethical. What characteristics do you associate with this person?

From my ethics workshops, I have compiled a summary of the lists received when participants are asked those questions. I call these the Ten Enduring or Universal Values. They are values for business executives, politicians, accountants and anyone else. These ethical principles are what people believe we mean by being ethical. Hopefully, this list represents a core that we have a consensus on. Consequently we will have a means of measuring the ethics of our decisions instead of saying, "Who's to decide?"

Honesty and Integrity

First, everyone in our Western culture believes in *honesty*. Honesty is an ethical value that is certainly better than dishonesty. Second is *integrity*—having the courage of one's convictions. Acting on principle rather than expediency is a virtue we all respect. However, integrity is not enough. Hitler had integrity. He had the courage of his convictions. One must have good convictions. Those people who blow with the wind, who are two-faced, who are hypocritical, and who will not stand for anything, stand for nothing.

Promise-Keeping

A third principle is *promise-keeping*. Note that promise keeping is different than honesty. Most promise-keeping problems occur after the promise is made. People may be honest in making a commitment but they may later break that promise. They may have all kinds of reasons and excuses for not following through but that doesn't mean they were dishonest when they made it. Promise-keeping has to do with keeping the commitment.

Fidelity

Fidelity or *loyalty* is the fourth principle. This is a difficult characteristic because we have so many loyalties. In fact, fidelity and loyalty are the cause of most ethical problems. Usually, it is the excuse you use to sacrifice one of the other nine principles. Ollie North was loyal to one cause, and as a result he was disloyal to many others. The real problem lies in sorting out loyalties and understanding what can legitimately be expected from you as a loyal person. Who are you loyal to? Is it the people in your firm, your clients? Who are your clients? Are they the people you're dealing with, or are they the board of directors, or the shareholders? This sorting process can be very difficult.

There are two concepts of loyalty in Malaysia. Dog loyalty and cat loyalty. Dogs are loyal to their master. Cats are loyal to the house. This can also apply in business and accounting contexts. One level and challenge of loyalty is in dealing with requests for help from the vice president of marketing, the CEO, or the CFO. One might be tempted to respond, "I owe loyalty to that person. He hired me. He is the one who negotiates my bills and rates." But is that the person or entity to whom you owe your loyalty as an accountant? No, he is not. How about the board of directors? What if the board of directors is acting in total self interest in a way that you think is wrong? Would you be tempted to say, "That's their decision." Actually, you owe nothing to this vague notion of the corporate entity. It's not even easy to say you owe it to the shareholders because today shareholders are just speculators for the most part. They don't have a sincere vested interest in the company, in most cases. They are just trading paper and trading futures. The fact is, one has to understand where their loyalty lies. Such loyalty becomes a major challenge for a person desiring to be ethical.

Fairness

Next on the list is *fairness*. Admittedly, we don't always know what fairness is. Consider the situation faced by a lawyer. One of the great excuses for some of the unseemly things done by lawyers is that, after all, no one knows what the truth is. Granted we may not always know the truth, but we do know what a lie is. Further, lawyers have no justification in trying to convince people of something that is untrue. We don't always know what is fair, but we often know what is unfair. And, we also know that we all should try to be fair. Can you imagine an ethical person who is not trying to be fair?

Caring

Sixth on the list is *caring for others*. In many ways, this characteristic absorbs all ten of the ethics principles. The most significant and probably dominant ethical rule is still the Golden Rule: Do unto others as you would have them do unto you. This encompasses such phrases as love thy neighbor, care about others, you are part of a community, and you are not an island unto yourself. If you didn't believe these phrases, why be honest? What difference does it make if you don't care about others—use them! They are like trees or rocks. The fact of the matter is that one of the great human conditions we have is natural compassion, caring, sense of community, and sense of family. In fact, philosophers well before Christianity, prescribed to the idea of 'do unto others.' In the Greek and Chinese philosophy, it was called the rule of reciprocity. "If you have trouble knowing how to treat other people, ask yourselves how would you like to be treated in that position." What a simple notion of empathy. Think of yourself as the person being lied to, rather than the liar and watch how your perspective shifts. The white-lie notion is simply nonsense. If the lie is so white and inconsequential, then theoretically, the other person wouldn't mind. Granted, some times they don't, but often they do. Further, we must recognize the social amenity lie where caring isn't even an assertion. Consider the question, "How are you?". "Fine." In a way you know it wasn't a real question so you didn't give a real answer. I was asked once, "Are you really telling me I should tell the truth at all times?" My reply was, "Yes, as much as you can." My colleague responded, "Well, suppose, for instance, my mother-in-law makes a pie that I hate. Every time I go to her house she feeds me the pie that she's so proud of and she says, 'Well, how do you like the pie?' Am I supposed to tell her the truth?" I said, "I think it would be better, kinder, and more respectful if you did." Why? Because what happens when you lie? First of all, it is not in your best interest. She continues to give you more pie. She may even send you an extra pie. In addition, she thinks she makes great pies so she offers pies to everybody. Similarly, if I ask you, 'How do I look today?' And you think to yourself, 'He looks like a clown, but I'll tell him he looks fine.' Then I go on TV looking like a clown. Thanks friend.

What is the basis of such lies? A lack of respect for the autonomy of the other person to make decisions about their own lives. And you have become a conspirator. For what? It is not the end of the world if you don't like the pie. Just say, "Sorry, Mom. I don't like it. Maybe other people do, but I'm not one of them." You could make statements like that but why don't you? Not to protect her feelings, but to avoid the confrontation. Most of the time these so-called white-lies are really designed to protect us from the hassle and the difficulty of being truthful.

Respect

Next on the consensus is *respect for others*. This is different than caring because although you may not even care about another, you may respect their autonomy and respect them as a human being. In considering this attribute, I recall some of my own weaknesses. As an employer one of the hardest things for me is personnel issues. Performance reviews and the like often prove to be terrible situations. In one particular case, a promotion possibility had arisen. The most likely candidate was a very capable young married woman who had just had a child. As I thought about her, I decided she would never want that job because it involved travel. It involved too many things that I decided she couldn't possibly want. It just wouldn't be good for her. Consequently, I never offered her the job—she never had the chance. Now, she may have turned it down. She may have agreed with me, but I realized years later how incredibly pretentious that decision was of me. How awful that was of me to make the choice for her rather than give her the opportunity to choose for herself. Further, I deprived her the pleasure of knowing that I esteemed her to be worthy of the position. That was a gift I had an opportunity to give and it was lost. Respect for others carries with it an understanding of how they feel.

Responsibility

Next, *responsible citizenship* requires participating, being law-abiding, and being someone who is part of a community.

Excellence

Ninth, the *pursuit of excellence* infers that we do our job well. Why is that an ethical principle? Well, for example, I don't understand all my investments and the tax consequences of each so I hire an accountant. I trust him to take care of my resources. He has an ethical obligation to be informed, to be prepared. It is more than just a competency issue, it is an ethical obligation which is no different than a surgeon who has an ethical obligation to be excellent.

Accountability

The final item on the list of ethical characteristics is *accountability*. The difficulty in professions such as law and accounting lies in determining how one can be both representational and accountable.

Each of these characteristics can be broken down into sophisticated subsets. Honesty involves truthfulness. It also involves non-deception which is different than truthfulness. And, in many cases, it involves candor, and in some cases it depends upon the nature of the relationship and whether or not you have an obligation to be forthright. It is precisely the application of those subtle principles, truthfulness, non-deception, and candor, that I urge you to explore. Consider them in the context of various relationships. What is your responsibility with the IRS as it relates to truthfulness, non-deception, and candor? What is your responsibility in relating to subordinates? What is your responsibility in selling a business to another. Are you responsible to the shareholders, or to the readers of your statements? These questions make a difference.

Promise-keeping not only has the notion of keeping the letter of the law, but also sometimes the spirit of the law. That is challenging with tax law because the spirit of the law means pay. In contrast your job as a tax accountant is not to pay. You must wrestle with this and establish some ground to stand on where you feel comfortable ethically in understanding that position.

Why We Are Not Ethical

Finally, I want to point out five major reasons why ethics is easier said than done. The first is self-deception. Be aware that one of the easiest things to say is, "This isn't ethics, this is business." A notion has developed that says, "I can check my ethics at the door and I don't have to apply ethical principles because I am in business." This is a double standard. Other familiar self-deception phrases are, "Everyone does it," "To get along, go along," or "You don't understand." This phrase assumes that if I knew what you knew I'd agree with you. Wrong! I can know everything you know and still disagree with you because I don't have the same interest that you do. What are other common rationalizations? "I can't do any good if I lose my job." "I have no time for ethical subtleties." "Ethics is a luxury I can't afford right now." "It's not my job." "It's not my worry." "It's not my problem." Here is where self-deception is blatant and reform is vital. It's always your problem. Moreover, we make our own problems by not speaking up. For instance, the CFO who is presented with the option of altering the books in effect sees only a black and white option. I either cheat and run all the risks incumbent therein, or I lose my job and the company goes down the tubes. What the CFO forgot to do was shift the burden back. It isn't his problem.

There is a story of a man who wakes up in the middle of the night, pacing back and forth, and his wife asks, "What is the matter, Harry?" He answers, "I owe George $5,000 and I don't have it. I don't know what to do." His wife immediately picks up the phone and says, "Hello George. I'm sorry to call at four in the morning but about that money we owe you, we don't have it. Good night." After she hangs up the husband says, "What in the world did you do that for?" Then she reasoned, "Look, now it's his problem. Come to bed." The point is when you take the ethical problem upon yourself you have to make the decision. Instead, shift it back saying, "I won't do it. So are you really going to fire me?" Do you know how difficult it is to fire somebody who insists on not lying? That is not a strong position to be in. Granted he could do it subtly, over the long haul but only if you're both still around. On the other hand, if you go along with him, you certainly won't be around because you'll be in jail with him. Avoid making your own problems.

Self-Indulgence

Self-indulgence is the second reason why ethics is easier said than done. Selfishness continually assaults the conscience with temptations and rationalizations. Many who lie break commitments. Violators of laws say, "I'm doing it for my family. I'm creating jobs." This is called vicarious selfishness. In such situations, you can't do for others what you can't do for yourself.

Self-Protection

Next on the list is self-protection. This defense is evident in Watergate, in the Iran Contra affair, and in our own lives. You didn't want to do anything wrong, but now you have. The mistake has been made and you've got to cover it up. One cover-up leads to another; it's a slippery slope and we just don't want to pay the piper. As a result, through self-protection, we get on a cycle.

Self-Righteousness

Fourth, self-righteousness is verbalized by the statement, "I am certain I am right." This moral imperialism occurred when Ollie North said, "I know what is good for this country," and every other American's rights were rejected.

Faulty Reasoning

Surprisingly, the fifth reason is simply faulty reasoning. We must teach people to estimate the costs and risks of their decisions. I have found almost invariably that people overestimate the costs of being ethical. "I'll lose my job. I'll lose the election. I'll lose the account. Terrible things will happen." Sometimes the consequences are terrible but often they're not. On the other hand, people always underestimate the costs of being unethical. "No one will know," or "I'll deal with it when it comes up." We should be teaching people to think out their actions, and to rationalize in effective, constructive ways.

Conclusion

Finally, and in conclusion, there are going to be times when you feel like a salmon swimming upstream. You'll be tempted to say, "This is nonsense. I can't do this. I can't be the only one trying to be ethical." I suggest you remember the words of Edmund Hale who said, "It is true I am only one person; but I am one. And the fact that I cannot do everything will not prevent me from doing all that I can do."

Questions

1. In what ways does the idea of the "survival of the fittest" contradict the idea of ethics?
2. For what reasons has the accountant been considered the most honest professional in business? Is this perspective changing?
3. What are the challenges of ethics in business today? Are they different for the accounting profession?
4. What is the moral imperative in business? In reality? How do they differ?
5. What does ethics mean?
6. Who is the most ethical person you know? What makes them ethical?

7. What are the ten enduring or universal values of ethics? Do you believe they are all part of being "ethical"?
8. Should ethics be based upon the spirit or the letter of the law?
9. Because something is legal, does that mean it is ethical?
10. Why is an acceptance of ethics easier said than done? How is selfishness involved in unethical behavior?

2
Ethical Issues in the Practice of Accounting _____

ROBERT J. SACK
Mr. Sack is a graduate of Miami University (Ohio). He is a lecturer in accounting at the Darden School, the University of Virginia. Previously he was the chief accountant of the SEC's Enforcement Division and a partner of Touche Ross and Co. He is a member of the AICPA, the AAA and the Ohio and New York state CPA societies.

Introduction _____

"We believe that professionals will have a stronger personal code when they come together to discuss issues of right and wrong that affect them professionally." A primary reason that we study and think about ethical issues is to inspire individuals to think through the consequences of their actions in advance. As a result, we will be more likely to have a firm personal conviction for what we believe.

In addition, we learn from people who have been trying to get ethical codes into place where we work. Their successes and failures provide a sound model for us to follow. Building on this foundation, there is a third explanation of why we talk about the problems of our profession. We need such interaction because the field of accounting is objective and neutral, and we pride ourselves on our objectivity, our coolness and our search for the truth. Consequently, we can easily become disconnected from the reality of our businesses. We can easily become disconnected from the moral choices that are involved in what we do. We can easily become amoral.

In working towards these three goals, first let me describe specific situations that I've observed, particularly after working three years in Washington D.C. Let me also share with you some issues faced by the American Accounting Association, the association of those that teach, as they face questions such as: how can we teach more than just accounting, how can we work into a lesson on cash the difference between right and wrong, and moral codes? You might think that it is easy to simply say, "Every professor ought to go

_____
Reprinted by permission of Robert J. Sack.

beyond GAAP and teach about what flows from the way such rules are applied." I can assure you that not every professor finds him/herself content to step up to that job. Thirdly, we will consider the situations that confront us in our daily practice and ask ourselves, "What do those things imply for the way we conduct our lives and the way we conduct our firms?"

Definition of Ethical Goals

For purposes of discussion, we ought to define some goals. What is it that we are trying to accomplish here? The list is long, but it boils down to: do unto others as you would have them do unto you. For accountants, however, our code should hold us to the test of how we respond to the expectations of our group, the group in which we work and live. We will discuss further this issue of whose expectations we must meet, what they expect of us, and how we react if we don't want to respond to those expectations.

After talking with groups about this subject, let me stress the deep human pain that I have seen when the law brings some kind of action against a CPA. Words can't express the bitter humiliation that stems from the statement, "We think you have violated the law and we're going to disbar you from practicing." Those are painful experiences.

Let me describe something that happened a week or two ago. I attended a function to talk about the way corporations have adopted codes of ethics within their firms, in order to keep their firms from faltering. During the meeting, a defense representative announced his purpose for attending by saying, "My CEO said, `I do not want this company hauled down to D.C. to be forced to testify on procurement, etc. I do not want to be accused of immoral business behavior. I want something done.' Then the CEO, turning to his CFO and staff said, `You figure out how to help us avoid that problem.' The response was, `Look, we've got 75,000 employees in 100 locations all over the world. How are we going to assure that all 75,000 adhere to a company-wide code so that these individuals don't embarrass the firm?'" They now have a book that outlines a code of ethics and includes an 800 number where you may call if (1) you feel pressured to step beyond the code, or (2) you see a friend or colleague wavering with ethical issues.

That representative went on to say, "It is my job to man that phone. I received 350 phone calls the first year and 400 the second year." Interestingly, seven or eight of those phone calls had to do with the misstating of financial statements. Other callers said, "I'm charging my time to this job, but this job already has too much time charged to it. I'll charge my time to another job which has just begun and no one will know." That is a big problem in the defense contracting business. Based on the knowledge gained from phone calls, this representative described a wonderful network that they had built. A code that everyone slashed their wrists and signed up to. This was admirable because although many corporations solve their culture problem by establishing a code of conduct for their people, few ever enforce it. I never saw anybody who said, "We're going to see that it actually takes place." For the remainder of the conference we discussed this issue of enforcement.

In thinking about this company later, however, I said to myself, "What is their principle business?" It occurred to me that out of the 75,000 people, 50,000 are in the defense business making nuclear bombs. And I said, "Congratulations. We now have a purely strong moral basis on which to build nuclear weapons." There is something incongruous about this statement that hit me hard. The pact was twofold. First, it pointed out to me how narrow one's scope can be. It really takes a new perspective, a going away, to stand back and say, "What is the larger picture? What is the real ethical question here?" That is very difficult. The second is, each of us, regardless of how strong we feel about doing right and adhering to our own code, have moral holes in our own makeup. We are all vulnerable somewhere.

Ethics in Accounting and Society

With that sense of humility, then, let's look at ethics in accounting as it relates to society, the profession, and our individual client situations. More specifically, this approach will address ethics first, in response to the expectations of society, second, in our response to our profession, and third in the way we respond to the specific jobs in which we find ourselves.

As experts in accounting, control and cool figuring, we tend to focus only on the facts. The answers are clear because the mathematics demonstrate to us the solution. For example, I taught a class once, where we were discussing fixed costs, the distinction between fixed costs and valuable costs, and why anybody would care. I called on a student and said, "Won't you come to the blackboard and show us your description of a fixed cost." The student went to the board and drew a little chart. I said, "Now, can you demonstrate to me what happens when the sales curve crosses that fixed curve." He replied, "That is break-even point!" He went to the board and drew the break-even point and drew the appropriate curve. I had a feeling of accomplishment; real understanding was taking place in the classroom. Then I said, "Now, you are the CEO of the third biggest car firm in the United States and you are seeing that the sales demand curve is encroaching on your fixed costs. What do you do?" The student replied, "I know what to do. Just like Iacocca, I reduce fixed costs, right?" The class said, "Exactly right! Reduce fixed costs." We understood all of those concepts. I went home feeling good; what a dynamite class that was.

However, in preparing for the next day's class I realized that we didn't talk about the effects of reducing fixed costs. My accounting students understood the accounting framework very well, but we didn't in any way talk about the consequences of altering fixed costs. This additional issue needed to be brought to their attention. After considering the fixed costs and the decision is made to shut down that plant, what happens to the people? Don't tell me what happens to the firm as a result of all those people, now unemployed, who can't buy your cars. Instead, give thought to your role as Chief Executive Officer over the people who have worked for you for 15 years. Is this not an element of the wonderful standard accounting measures? Do you not have to say, "I have an obligation to those people as well"? I believe society expects expert accountants to include such nonaccounting events as factors in the critical decisions that we make.

Ethics in Business

In the professional world, accountants are heavily relied upon in the area of control. Clients call and say, "I'm having a hard time. I can't meet my goals. Help me figure out a way to design both controls and systems to help my people stay on track." That is one thing accountants do well. As experts in controls, it is essential that we consider: to what degree do our control systems drive people to do things which destroy themselves and destroy their companies.

Not long ago, the Securities and Exchange Commission raised a wonderful case against a company called AMI. It was a sleepy little old firm, just barely making it, when a man named Roy Ash took charge. He said, "I'm going to make this a go-go company. And pretty soon, instead of EPS of 10:1, it's going to be 40:1. We're all going to get rich." In turning AMI around, he brought in a bunch of high powered people and the company as a whole, not just Mr. Ash, adopted a policy called NBO. Essentially, that meant that you and I agree on what your goals are going to be for your division next year, then I leave you alone to manage toward those goals. Implied in NBO was the idea that it was a fair goal to start with. However, as it turned out, Mr. Ash leaned on managers at the start of the year and said, "Look, we're all going to earn $1.90 a share next year. Your share of that is $.42." As the year went along periodic meetings occurred. If a manager was not on target at $.42 a share quarterly, the manager would be told, "If you can't find a way to manage that goal, we'll find someone else who can." Now this statement does not need to be repeated many times until that manager finds a way to manage towards his goals.

One of the ways AMI did this was to say, "Who cares when you cut the books off. I mean, a sale is a sale, right? Does it really matter whether we reach a little bit into next week and take some of the sales we ship next week and put it in this week? After all, it was all made during this month anyway." Soon, one week stretched into two weeks, then three, until eventually it wasn't too hard to say, "We know that customer is going to buy it eventually, let's book it now." Consequently, AMI managed toward their objectives rather than towards reality, until finally they were so far beyond reality that the company collapsed from its own weight.

It is easy to blame the system for an individual failure when in actuality we need to hold ourselves responsible for our own actions. However, one of the actions that we are responsible for, as accountants, is creating those very systems which measure people. We have an ethical obligation to consider the effect that our systems will have on people.

Ethics in Our Jobs

Thirdly, experts in accounting have an obligation to ensure that accounting serves society and not the companies for whom they work. We are reminded of the disaster that has faced us all with regard to the thrifts. Unfortunately, case by case, there will be some accountants who will be accused of having shut their eyes to bad loans. This leads into a much broader issue which we as accountants share. We now have a new FASB statement that says thrifts should not take into income, at the time they sign the loan, fees that they receive in cash. Those fees should be spread over the life of the loan.

To illustrate, when you take out a loan, the bank asks for cash up front, reasoning that they've got so many front-end costs. Besides, they intend to sell the loan, probably at the risk of taking a loss. To compensate, the bank will charge you three points plus extra fees to close the deal, not to mention investigation fees. As it turns out, they were taking those fees into income at the time the loan was signed. Factors such as how good the loan is or how long it is kept, became unimportant. Consequently, these financial institutions were no longer in the business of making loans. Instead, they were in the business of writing loans and then getting rid of them quickly. The basic characteristics of the loan process became obsolete, as banks concentrated on simply writing out as many loans as possible. To the extent that this endeavor was successful, the front-end fees produced earnings and capital which kept the FSLIC satisfied.

Directing the focus back to the FASB statement, it should be obvious that such a statement was unnecessary. It all boiled down to a need for just two or three CFOs, and two or three CPAs to say, "I know what the revenue recognition process for a thrift is, and just because you've got it in cash doesn't make it income. If it's part of the income earned by the loan, it ought to be spread over the life of the loan." A few responsible people were needed to stand up and preclude special exceptions for an industry just because they were in need at the time. The accounting profession didn't need that statement. They simply needed a few people to stand up and react to the expectations of our society.

Standards Overload in Accounting

Ethical issues also arise with respect to an accountant's obligation to the profession and the expectations evident in the profession. A major concern in accounting deals with standards overload. We have too many rules, too many laws. As a result, the entire business society, including accountants, looks for laws as a way to avoid having to make a decision by themselves. However, it is not the FASB's fault that we have too many rules, nor is it the SEC's fault. It's our fault—yours and mine—and it's our responsibility to say, "I won't let it go any further. Regardless of the position others take, I won't allow this situation to continue."

As an example, consider the following. A large firm employed three young men to work on what was thought to be a very promising project. After a couple of years, however, the firm scratched the whole idea due to the lack of return and directed the men to work on a new project. But, determination would not let the men give up; this project had great potential. Only the short-sighted corporate entity stood in their way.

Finally, the three of them left the firm, pooled their cash, and started their own business to exploit this wonderful new idea. They hired a lawyer and a CPA and they said, "We've each pledged $100,000 to this firm. We figure it will take us three years to develop it, and we're going to spend about $100,000 per year. So, at the end of three years we will have spent all the money that we've had, but by then this project will be ready to go." The CPA said, "Before you continue let's consider the situation. Each of you will invest $100,000 into the firm, and the firm will lose it all in the first three years of operation, right? When you die, 100 years from now, you'll still have the basis of $100,000. Isn't it a shame not to find some way to take advantage of those losses personally, right now, rather than passing it on to your heirs?

I've got a better idea. Of the $300,000, put $100,000 in the corporation as the lawyer suggests. Then put $200,000 in a partnership which the three of you will own. Next, have the partnership undertake the R&D work, but contract with the corporation to do the R&D work on the partnership's behalf. In effect, the corporation retains the

$200,000 in cash because it bills the partnership for the work performed. Somehow that must be treated as a sale. At the end of the three years, the corporation has $300,000 in net worth and $200,000 worth of income. As for the partnership, they just lost $200,000 and each of the partners has a great loss."

Now, the accountant felt a sense of achievement not only because of this great tax idea, but because of the financial statements as well. Think about what could be done if this scenario was expanded. Think about what publicly-held companies would like to do if they could, instead of undertaking the R&D expenses and having all those huge losses they could just form partnerships of the Board of Directors and do the R&D on their behalf. Instead of having R&D expense, income would result.

Currently, there is a FASB Statement which says, "If you have R&D work conducted for a partnership or some other firm that is closely connected with the corporation itself, it's not income, but it's the corporation's expense." Why do we have such a FASB Statement? Isn't it pretty logical to deduce the substance of the event from the situation itself? The reason we have a FASB Statement is because there were enough practitioners and CFOs who said, "Oh, that's a clever idea." They did not have the ethical stamina to say, "No, that's not what the profession expects of me." A topic worth pursuing ought to involve an analysis of every FASB Statement to determine how many of those statements were unnecessary and were only written in order to help individuals do their jobs.

A New Code of Ethics

Fortunately, the accounting professionals instituted a new code of ethics. It's hard and it's tough and one of its most important attributes is that due care has now been defined. Although it was always there before, now the new code specifically states that by expressing due care you will do work that you are competent to do. Inherent in this commitment is the ability to recognize when to seek help because a job is beyond your capabilities. To go one step further, as a profession we have an ethical responsibility to finally acknowledge that passing the exam and becoming a CPA does not qualify each of us to actively perform all of the duties of a CPA. There is an increasing need for specialization.

When I worked at the SEC, one of our staff people had a CPA who had been called by somebody who picked his name out of the book and said, "You're a CPA?" "Yep." "I've got a form 10. I need somebody to sign his name to it." And this CPA said, "What's a form 10?" The client knew that he had it made right there. He said, "Don't worry about it. Come down here and we'll help you through it." The CPA didn't know what a form 10 was, he didn't know what GAAP was, and he didn't know was GAAS was. However, he was a very good tax practitioner. In frustration someone asked him, "You do know what GAAP is, don't you?" This fellow looked at him and said, "Yea, that's the stuff that the APB writes." He's not a bad or despicable man. However, for obvious reasons, he's no longer a CPA. Accountants need to find a way to say to society, "The range of responsibilities is big and no one of us is really capable of fulfilling that entire scope."

Responsibilities of Management

Let me consider one more idea concerning specific actions of CPAs and CFOs. A recent case from the SEC involved a CFO, 48 years old, who was hired into a new firm in March. The CEO said, "Come work with us. We're going to take over Hoover while they're asleep because we make the best vacuum sweepers in the world." It was a deal too good to pass up. The only problem was this great vacuum sweeper was hurried to the market too fast. The belt comes off. Now, a person doesn't mind getting down on hands and knees once to put the belt back on, but when it happens every week, it gets upsetting and customers want their money back.

As December approached, the stores were returning the sweepers in droves and sales were rapidly declining. Because the Chairman thought the marketplace expected a certain level of performance from the company, he ordered the CFO to find a way to deal with these returns. After being there only nine months, the CFO's solution was to simply ignore them. He figured out a way to process the returns without recording them in the books. This enabled the firm to meet its six and nine month sales goals along with achieving its forecasted income. However, when the nine month results were released, it wasn't quite enough. The CEO wanted to find a way to get a little more sales, a little more income, because "The market expects it of us."

The result was a system which created new transactions based upon the mere expectation of sales. Unfortunately, when the end of the year came sales still didn't meet expectations. The solution: reduce costs of goods sold. As a result, the company put out year-end statements at the end of June and the market was pleased. As the two guys looked at each other they said, "This obviously can't go on. We're going to have to face up to the returns because we don't have the cash. We're going to have to face up to the fact that we've reached into the next year for sales because we can't match it next year."

They decided together, one Sunday afternoon, to announce to the market that the financial statements were misstated possibly due to a programming error or computer blow up. Notably, they never did, at that point, bring themselves to say, "We misled the marketplace."

Finally, of course, the whole scheme collapsed after the CFO had only been employed for 18 months. Now the corporation is bankrupt. The expectations of the market may have been that the company report sales and income of a certain amount, but the expectations of the financial community were that the CFO would say to his new boss, "No, I'm not going to be unethical and I'm not going to let you be dishonest either. I'm not going to let you do that to yourself or to this business."

Finally, the E.F. Hutton case illustrates an issue concerning ethics and cash. Hutton, of course, deals with a large amount of cash because every branch takes in money from clients which it promises to send to New York and invest on their behalf. Or, one brings in stocks and expects to get cash back because the sale takes place. Hutton had figured out that the banking world was full of various time lags and they determined that clients didn't really know or care whether stock paid with a check was drawn on a San Francisco bank or New York bank. The idea was simple: a check was written and cashed at a bank. It then takes three or four days or more to float across the United States and then get back to the Hutton account where it was written. They even created an entire department to manage the float. Eventually, the pressure within Hutton became so great that it was more profitable to manage the float than it was to sell securities—and some of the divisions got carried away. They weren't simply investing the float, they were investing the bank's float.

At the end of the year, Hutton showed negative cash of $950 million and the financial statements were technically correct. Now, every accounting professor knows how to tell his students what to do with negative cash. It's an overdraft. The financial statements showed no cash and $950 million of overdraft. Evidently, nobody in the company, especially the accounting stream of people said, "How can we have almost a billion dollars in negative cash? Is it possible that we are illegally, or at least immorally borrowing from a bank who doesn't realize they are being borrowed against?" Recognize that when you teach cash, rather than simply having your students recognize how to handle the bank accounts, urge them to consider the ethical implications of management practices. This reverts back directly upon the opening paragraphs of this chapter and can be summarized in one statement.

Conclusion

Ethics for accountants has to do with the way individuals respond to the expectations of the community and, perhaps more importantly, the way they express their search for those expectations. Look for them; raise your sights and say, "What does society expect me to do in this situation?"

Questions

1. How can accounting procedures and ethics conflict? Provide some examples.
2. Are accountants responsible for non-accounting concerns? Why? What are some examples of non-accounting concerns which accountants should be aware of? What would you do if they occurred because of your actions?
3. What is behind the idea of a "standards overload"?
4. As an accountant, are you more responsible to your profession or to society? Will this change? Under what circumstances might your responsibility change?

3
Ethical Issues in the Practice of Accounting

WILLIAM D. HALL

Mr. Hall graduated from the University of Illinois with a master's degree in accountancy. He is a retired partner of Arthur Andersen & Co. and is presently serving as a consultant to Arthur Andersen's Business Ethics Program. After working in the Chicago World Headquarters, he moved to London, England, to serve as accounting and audit practice director for Europe and South Africa.

Introduction

Given my background, I shall direct my comments to ethics as it relates directly to auditors who examine and attest to financial statements and other financial data. The following chapters will discuss the ethical issues that are particularly relevant to those who prepare financial statements and to those who provide tax and consulting services, although many of the basic concepts have universal applicability.

Further, I shall address the need for strengthening the ethical environment in which we practice rather than dealing with specific ethical issues — for example, scope of practice. As important and controversial as some of these issues are, I am increasingly convinced that a major problem today is our preoccupation with details while giving inadequate attention to the basic objectives that underlie our practice. Too often, in our concern over ethical lapses, we attack symptoms rather than addressing root causes.

The basic ethical imperative for auditors is objectivity — or, as we more frequently express it, independence. To be independent, the auditor must never lose sight of the commitment to call the shots as he or she sees them. That is why we are members of a profession. As practitioners, we must subordinate our commercial instincts and our desire to be helpful to clients to our overriding responsibility for impartially reporting on presentations of financial statements and

Reprinted by permission of William D. Hall.

other data. In carrying out this responsibility, we must remain scrupulously free from bias or control in any form. When we act in this manner, we are **independent in fact** — the aspect that I wish to focus on today. Appearance of independence is an important subject, raising complex, sensitive and contentious issues, but that is grist for another mill.

Professional Ethics is an Aspect of One's Moral Values _____

By identifying the scope of my comments and providing my definition of professional ethics at the outset, I am not suggesting that professional ethics is something apart — something that the professional person dons as he or she enters the office and then hangs up upon leaving for the day. Indeed, such an attitude may underlie much of today's ethical confusion. Ethics is a way of life, involving the whole person and becoming an almost instinctive way of dealing with the moral ambiguities that confront us daily in our lives. It is not something that can be compartmentalized — turned on or off as situations demand. Stated another way, observance of professional ethics is but one aspect of one's moral code. I would never have much confidence in a person's professional ethics — when push comes to shove — if I had reservations about his or her ethics in general.

Know Yourself

To behave ethically, one must know oneself. A person must have a sense of his or her worth as a human being and a healthy, functioning set of values. A professional must understand and respect his or her role, not losing sight of it in the competing pressures that are inherent in modern society. The CPA certificate must be more, much more, than a license to earn a good living.

One of our greatest risks in addressing ethics is treating it as something apart — a matter covered, perhaps, by a written code and dealt with as a matter of compliance. As such, ethics becomes mechanical, perhaps even negative — a series of "thou shalt not's" — rather than a constructive, integral part of every action. We may even tend to think of it rather simplistically as observing rules aimed at avoiding the appearance of unacceptable acts that most of us would never do anyway — using inside information to invest in a client's stock or receiving gifts or other favors from a client, to cite two examples. We may not think as much about it being an ethical issue when:

- We discover an error in our work that has been used by others and remain silent, hoping it will not be discovered and rationalizing that it is probably too late for correction anyway;

- We close our eyes to corner-cutting by associates, telling ourselves that it is not important enough to create a ruckus and that it is really not our responsibility anyway;

- We help a client manipulate the rules without breaking them to achieve reported results that we know are not quite what they should be.

Rules and Data Overload May Obscure Ethical Issues

Often, as a reminder and a help in interpretation, rules provide guidance — for example, in our society generally, the Ten Command-ments and, at the level of our profession, the Code of Professional Conduct of the American Institute of Certified Public Accountants. But these rules are sterile indeed if people are not imbued with the spirit that lies behind them. At the worst, they invite legalistic hair-splitting and foster gamesmanship.

In many ways, this is analogous to what happens in organized religion. Nothing could be more important than a person's beliefs about the nature of the world — its origin and purpose and his or her role in it. Organized religions exist to perpetuate their adherents' doctrines, using creeds and other forms to focus the attention of their followers and others in fundamental tenets and to ensure faithful transmittal to future generations. But for many people, the traditions and rituals become the actuality; the form overshadows the substance. They lose sight of the underlying truths and what these should mean in their lives, and they tend to believe that observing the formalities fulfills their obligations. So it sometimes is with professional ethics as it relates to the practice of examining and reporting on financial data — the primary role of the auditor.

I emphasize that at the outset because a meaningful observance of ethics, of which our professional ethics is only one aspect, requires a thoughtful focus on one's role. We must not get lost in the details that tend to inundate us in today's complex, fast-moving society. In that connection, I would like to share some excerpts from a recent feature article in the *Chicago Tribune*:

"Information Anxiety": Its Effect on Individuals

Richard Saw Wurman, an architect, graphic designer and futurist, has identified a malady he believes to be at epidemic levels in this culture. He called it "information anxiety."

> It is a feeling you get when you realize you will never keep up with everything that you think you should know. There is too much to read, review, and to learn and never enough time.

It is a condition that evokes panic, listlessness, and guilt. In severe cases you may imagine yourself buried under a huge pile of newspapers, magazines, books, business reports, professional journals, instruction manuals, investment advice, application forms, and brochures.

Information anxiety is a term that opens a catalogue of complaints. It is not just the magnitude of written material that seems so overwhelming. You also are hopelessly behind in seeing the movies you ought to see, and you have been forgetting to tape that [PBS] series on ethics that a friend urged you to watch. You even missed two installments of "Lonesome Dove."

Quoting from Wurman's book, the article notes that "meaning is garbled and language eroded by babble, bromides, banality, sarcasm, superficiality and evasions." It goes on to observe: "A weekday edition of the *New York Times* contains more information than the average person was likely to come across in a lifetime in 17th Century England." Further, "more new information has been produced in the last 30 years than in the previous 5,000. About 1,000 books are published internationally every day, and the total of all printed knowledge doubles every year."

Does this recitation strike a responsive note? Does even hearing about the situation, and thinking about what lies ahead, exhaust — almost numb — you? But, you may wonder, aside from the brief reference to the television series on ethics, what it has to do with "Ethical Issues in Accounting" — the title of this chapter. A great deal, I am increasingly convinced. We are part of this overload, and our approach in coping has compounded the problem. It has tended to cause us, along with the rest of society, to lose our bearings.

The National Reliance on Laws, Regulations, and Rules

As a nation, we attempt to solve our ills with laws, regulations and rules. When one of these does not work, we try to patch it with more of the same. We accountants have experienced an almost geometric explosion of rules — those that we have created and those that have been imposed on us by others. The scope, size and sophistication of business itself have expanded greatly; the ever-changing financial techniques spawned by the brightest MBAs who have been attracted to investment banking in recent years challenge the accountant's ability to understand and evaluate intricate transactions and complex financial instruments.

To help the profession stay abreast, the American Institute of Certified Public Accountants and the Financial Accounting Standards Board have deluged the practitioner with a virtual flood of authoritative practice standards. Up to 1948 when I entered practice, the

Committee on Accounting Procedures had issued only 37 relatively simple, non-binding Accounting Research Bulletins. In April, 1987, when I last made a tabulation (it would be worse today), a practitioner had to be at least aware of the following information sources that are currently effective and in use:

- 6 Accounting Research Bulletins
- 26 Accounting Principles Board Opinions
- 85 FASB Statements of Financial Accounting Standards
- 229 Interpretations of the foregoing bulletins' opinions and statements
- 38 FASB Technical Bulletins
- 6 FASB Concepts Statements
- 21 AICPA Statements of Position
- 147 Issues addressed by the FASB Emerging Issues Task Force
- 7 Governmental Accounting Standards Board Statements
- 4 GASB Interpretations and Bulletins

Authoritative auditing statements have grown apace. The profession's code of professional conduct supplemented by numerous pronouncements of the securities and exchange commission, presents the profession with a continually increasing set of behavioral rules that he or she must understand and comply with.

With all these rules, we are prone to lose sight of what our work is all about. We cannot see the forest for the trees; the rules become an end in themselves. We come to regard compliance with a code, for example, as what ethics is all about.

The subtle but pervasive risk is a casual, almost cynical, attitude toward accounting, the role of financial statements in society, that lets the accountant or auditor accept — even devise — something that does not quite pass the smell test merely because it seems to be within the rules — or, at least, is not proscribed by the rules. When he or she does this, it is much a lack of independence — a bias toward taking the easy way out to accommodate a client's desires — as is the flagrant case that turns on a direct financial interest. Especially with the competitive pressures that exist today, insensitivity to the underlying substance of professional ethics on the part of the individuals and firms could be the greatest threat to the future of the profession. It could sap the profession's strength, its credibility, its very reason for being.

Accountants of Fifty Years Ago Faced Fewer Dilemmas _____

It is tempting — if somewhat unrealistic — to hearken back to the "good old days." Much of our longing for a simpler time when life was less complex and, perhaps, there were fewer moral ambiguities is little more than nostalgia. The passing years have a way of creating a golden aura around even the worst of times. One has only to read some of the books about the Great Depression to see this.

But it is true that the proliferation of accounting and reporting rules over the last three decades, coupled with the growing complexity of business, has aggravated the problem. The auditor of the 1940s and earlier had relatively few rules to follow; it came naturally for him or her, therefore, to get down to basics — what appeared to be the best answer. In the light of today's complexity, the auditors of 50 years ago may have been naive, and sometimes wrong, but they were plagued by fewer doubts and uncertainties. And, with less significance attached to performance trends and earnings per share, clients offered less resistance even when they might not agree.

The Accounting Practice of Yesterday

A major element in my firm's culture is the story, told over and over again (and possibly embellished), about how, when we were much smaller, we gave up the audit of one of the country's preeminent corporations because we would not yield on a matter, as I recall, of balance-sheet classification. We all took pride, too, from having resigned clients in two major industries in the 1950s because we did not believe that their accounting was right — even though sanctioned by "generally accepted accounting principles." In the absence of detailed pronouncements, disagreements over accounting matters tended to be debated on the basis of perceptions of right or wrong.

The Accounting Practice of Today

How different practice is today! The intricate network of rules, some so complex as to require even experienced accountants to seek consultation with experts, tends to make accountants and auditors focus on the rules themselves rather than on the substance that lies behind them. And companies, particularly larger ones, frequently have a sophisticated understanding of these rules and the impact on their earnings, ratios and other performance indicators that are so important today.

With this situation prevailing, it becomes easy for accountants and auditors to regard the rules as ends in themselves and to see nothing wrong in finding ways to avoid them without breaking them. Anyone participating now in discussions with clients about the accounting to be followed for a transaction must be well-briefed on the rules and how other companies have dealt with purportedly similar situations. The question of what is the best answer may never come up — or, if it does, is quickly brushed aside. This is why some competent, otherwise conscientious auditors consider it constructive client service to find ways around the very standards their firms have urged the Financial Accounting Standards Board to adopt — a subtle but crucial difference from sanctioning or even pointing out a free choice among specifically permitted alternatives.

We Must Focus Directly on Ethics

But important as it is to establish the underpinning — to have people sensitive to the objectives of what they are doing — we cannot overlook the need to focus directly on ethics. I might not always have said this; I might have shared the rather widespread view that one learns ethics early — at home, at church and in school — and that it is too late to change a person's mindset when he or she becomes an adult. What I have read and heard during the last few years, however, has changed my mind. Although it is true that "as the twig is bent, the tree grows," one's early conditioning can be modified — reinforced and strengthened by additional experience and training. Indeed, there is a growing belief among some experts that worklife can have as profound an influence on adult adjustment as childhood.

We need to sensitize people to moral issues and ambiguities. We should be more concerned, perhaps, about the person who passes by a moral dilemma without recognizing it than we are about the person who consciously and callously commits a wrong. In the long run, moral insensitivity could be our biggest problem. People must be aware that virtually everything they do — or don't do — has an ethical implication.

They must learn to live with ambiguity — and that bothers accountants, who want a clear answer to everything. Most of the ethical issues we confront are not starkly clear; they appear in varying shades of gray. A problem may have no obvious answer, or it may arguably be too immaterial to concern oneself about. The most insidious ethical dilemmas I have seen are situations in which persons acquiesce in something that may not be quite right but does not seem too important at the outset — then the problem grows and they find themselves deeply involved without any easy way out. It may be compounded by an unwillingness to confront or let down a superior or associate with whom one has had a close working relationship. Without being privy to the facts, I would suspect that that was the situation when the relatively minor figure, Lisa Jones, was convicted in a recent case involving Drexel Burnham — subject, I might note, to a stiffer mandatory minimum sentence than was received by either Ivan Boesky or David Levine.

Ethical Issues are Moral Issues

We must face up to the fact that ethical issues are moral issues. Modern society, unfortunately, seems to be uncomfortable, even embarrassed, addressing moral issues head on. In reaction, perhaps, to the excessive and sometimes hypocritical puritanism of earlier generations, we bend over backwards to avoid appearing judgmental. Rather than tell someone an action is wrong, we prefer to cop out by saying that it is against the rules, that it might lead to trouble or that someone might misunderstand it. By being passive, neutral, we foster an aura of moral ambiguity — at its worst, an attitude that something is wrong only if one is caught.

Of course, we do not wish to be narrow, insufferably self-righteous and arrogant in our judgments. After all, many issues are gray, at least around the edges, and we must respect sincerely held beliefs of others. We must, however, be sensitive to motivations, especially our own, and not erode the sharp edges of right and wrong to the point that we can rationalize away problems that should be addressed.

Our Ethical Responsibility

But who is responsible for increasing our ethical sensitivity — and how can they accomplish this. The responsibility rests, first and foremost, with use as individuals. Ethics is a personal matter, and we cannot pass the buck to others. Certainly society sometimes makes it difficult for one to behave ethically, but no one promised us an easy life — especially those of us who have accepted the challenge to be professionals.

The individual must consciously focus on ethical concerns. He or she must go beyond the rules, thinking about why the rules are necessary and written as they are — in other words, the substance behind the form.

I would encourage persons to read — broadly and well. We turn out superb technicians today, but too often their underpinning in philosophy and history is weak. A professor at a leading business school has developed a series of courses on leadership in which his students read and discuss novels, plays, poetry and books of criticism. In his view, research on leadership could be strengthened by a closer link to humanistic thought. Hoping that students will begin to see that there is no need to draw a sharp line between recreational reading and their business careers, he said, "In my grander fantasies, I imagine them seeing good literature as being almost as important to them as *The Wall Street Journal.*

From personal experience, I know that reading George Eliot's *Middlemarch* and vicariously experiencing the ethical trap into which one of the characters was walking helped me identify and resolve an issue that had been tugging at my subconscious.

Profession Must Focus on Its Objectives _____

The individual does, however, deserve support from others. One of these is the profession itself. A major way that we, as a profession, can help our members strengthen their ethics is to concentrate our attention on the objectives of our role and performance. We must remember what the purpose of financial reporting is. We must recall why society, through its representatives, licenses us to practice. We must be continuously conscious of the fact that our function is to exercise independent professional judgment in the public interest, not to follow rules blindly or to manipulate them to achieve some desired results.

I am not denigrating the importance of rules. Much as I might wish that we did not have so many and that some of those we have were easier to understand, I recognize the need. Society and business are becoming increasingly complex; that is the world in which we live, and we cannot opt out. We cannot be like the 11th century British King Canute, who stood at the water's edge and commanded the tide to recede.

The Need for Rules

We need rules to help us find our way through the maze of complex transactions and financial instruments. We need them to achieve a reasonable consistency in the exercise of professional judgment. We need them even as reminders: accountants and auditors, like human beings generally, are prone to rationalize the propriety of what they want to do, and they need rules to warn them about actions that might compromise the appearance, if not the fact, of independence.

But we need a compass. First and foremost, in my view, this calls for an integrated conceptual framework. We need to know what our accounting and financial reporting is for — what users want and need within the parameters of what accounting and reporting can provide. For present purposes, I do not propose even to suggest what that framework should be; I shall only note that it should be logical and persuasive, serving as a guide against which standards can be established and implemented. In other words, professionals need guidance in terms of objectives rather than having to rely almost exclusively on detailed rules. One can hardly generate much moral fervor about applying a standard that can be explained only in terms of its mechanics — for example, that in determining earnings per share, a convertible security is a common stock equivalent if, at the time of issuance, it has cash yield, based on market price, of less than 2/3 of the ten-current bank prime interest.

I must confess that I did not fully appreciate how pervasive our preoccupation with rules was until after I retired. It hit me while I was leading a graduate seminar on accounting concepts and attempting to get some bright students to broaden their vision and contemplate approaches outside our conventional cost-based model. How frustrating it was to get them to break out of the written rules — to envision something not covered by an FASB pronouncement! Some never did. Occasionally I would even get the reaction that we would be hurting net income or earnings per share by a change — as if our role is to enhance performance rather than to report, as best we can within accounting's inherent limitations, financial position and results of operations. Sometimes it even seemed that some students had no vision of accounting beyond applying a set of rules in such a way as to approach some desired results. And these were intelligent, honest people.

Schools Have a Vital Role

Schools, I believe, can do much to increase ethical sensitivities — and some are doing so. A number of outside individuals and organizations are funding or assisting in the design of programs to teach business ethics. I have been involved in one of these; and, while I readily acknowledge that there is no single or "best" way to approach this, I have developed a few ideas. Fortunately, not being an academician, I am not forced to face the nitty-gritty decisions involved in how much time should be allotted to what I recommend and what might have to be cut to make room for it. It is comfortable to be able to deal with concepts and leave to someone else the difficult tasks of implementation.

An integrated program should include all or part of three approaches: a course or segment of a course directed to ethics generally and business ethics specifically; case studies that integrate ethical dilemmas into a realistic business problem; and short vignettes that can be sprinkled throughout other studies to maintain or increase students' awareness of ethical issues.

Initially, I had some reservations about a course or part of a course that would focus primarily on ethics. I thought that business students might find it too abstract, too unrelated to the bottom line, to hold their attention. I was concerned that it might sound like preaching. And I feared that it might be viewed as the teacher's vehicle for indoctrinating students in his or her own set of values. All of those are valid concerns. I have discovered, however, that competent ethicists can be practical, and fascinating. Without pushing their own answers, they can raise students' awareness of ethical dilemmas and get them thinking. The only problems that I see are fitting this into an already crowded curriculum and finding qualified teachers. I could pass this off rather loftily by saying that it is a matter of priorities (is it more important to teach techniques or to foster ethical behavior?), but that would be offering a glib response to a real problem. The matter should, however, receive careful thought.

The case study approach is fine if the cases are well written and if the teacher is comfortable with the case approach. There can be a problem if a case focuses too heavily either on the functional problem or on the ethical issues, and achieving a good balance can be difficult. A good case will take at least one class session, and often more. Unless it has functional substance related to the course, a teacher may be unwilling to sacrifice that much time from the material he or she feels must be covered. A well-designed case, however, can generate a real-life feeling in dealing with ethical dilemmas.

Vignettes can serve a particularly useful purpose. My initial concern had been that ethical issues are often ambiguous, sneaking up on one as he or she works on a business problem, and that a vignette might be so simplistic as to be unreal. I underestimated the abilities of good writers and producers. Recently I have seen several vignettes that had me squirming in my chair and left me, even days later, thinking back and wondering what the person decided — and, more important, what I would have decided.

And finally, on the matter of education, I would strongly support curricula that place a greater emphasis on why's and less on what's. Students should be taught to think, not to parrot rules. They should be educated as professionals, not trained as technicians. School should offer an individual a challenging opportunity to think broadly, to know oneself and to prepare for one's role in society as a thoughtful, contributing member. It is obvious, I am sure, that I would place far greater stress on the humanities. In accounting education, I would focus more on what financial reporting is about than on highly specialized technical courses.

Companies Must Demonstrate Concern and Commitment

It would be unfair to suggest that individual practitioners and educators alone need to be made more sensitive to ethical imperatives. The same applies to professional firms and businesses. They must be as concerned with reinforcing the ethical training of their personnel as they are with updating their technical competence.

The focus should be on the substance of ethics, not just the form. In thinking back to training prepared when I was responsible for developing and administering independence standards at my firm, I regret that we focused primarily on the rules rather than on the underlying rationale. We told people what to do and — more often — what not to do, but we did not sufficiently stress the why's.

Many professional firms and businesses have issued codes of conduct — and this is important. Managements must, however, act in such a way as to leave no doubt in the minds of members and employees that they mean what they say, that they are totally committed to high ethical standards.

A professor who has run ethics workshops for a number of companies has pointed out that they must overcome an assumption by many employees that top management wants profits however they have to be achieved. Although I doubt whether personnel of auditing firms have such a cynical view about their organizations, the leaders may not always give them reason to believe that a concern about ethics is a high priority. A perception that management looks aside from a little corner-cutting by those who bring in quite a bit of business undermines the message that ethical behavior is all-important. The body language, if you will, may not always give enough support to the written codes of ethics.

Conclusion

I hope that the present attention to ethics awareness and education is not just a fad, spawned by the notorious insider-trading scandals that have buffeted Wall Street the last two or three years. The subject is far too important for that. As the first three articles of the Code of Professional Conduct begin:

- In carrying out their responsibilities as professionals, members should exercise sensitive professional and moral judgments in all their activities.

- Members should accept the obligation to act in a way that will serve the public interest, honor the public trust, and demonstrate commitment to professionalism.

- To maintain and broaden public confidence, members should perform all professional responsibilities with the highest sense of integrity.

Let us hope that members, when they refer to the code, spend some time reading and thinking about these concepts rather than turning immediately to the detailed rules. As individuals, as firms and as a profession, we must constantly keep in mind that ethical behavior, coupled with intelligent, competent service is the foundation of accounting and auditing. Responsibility to the public for objective financial reporting must always come first. Only if we demonstrate this by our behavior will the profession maintain the credibility needed for its existence.

Questions

1. What is "information anxiety", and how are you affected by it?
2. Why have accountants been inundated with a large amount of rules and regulations? How could an increased understanding of ethics reduce this need?

3. How could moral insensitivity become the accounting profession's biggest problem? Is it already occurring? If so, in what ways? How can it be reversed?
4. Who is responsible for the needed increase in ethical sensitivity?
5. What is an accountant's role — to evaluate a company's performance or to report on a company's financial situation?
6. What approaches should be integrated into an ethics program? Do you agree?
7. How can individual professionals keep an interest in ethics from becoming a passing fad?

4
The New AICPA Code
of Ethics

GEORGE D. ANDERSON

Mr. Anderson graduated with great distinction from Stanford University in 1947. He recently chaired the Anderson Committee that rewrote the AICPA's code of ethics. In the past he has served as treasurer of the National Governor's Conference and has been president of the Montana Society of CPAs. He has been selected as the CPA of the Year in Montana and was recently awarded the 1988 AICPA Gold Medal for Distinguished Service to the profession.

Introduction

Ethics has become a most important subject during the last few years. Although the concept was an extremely important one in the past, it received very little publicity and problems were generally taken care of in the organization or association within which a member failed to follow ethical rules.

Generally, we have been like Calvin and Hobbs — ethics are for the other fellow — what I do is okay because, in my opinion, I do it in an ethical manner. However, we need to monitor and police that fellow down the street because he does not follow the standards the way I would like him to.

In the past, the concentration in ethics has been on how we treated our professional colleague, rather than how we treated the public. More recently, on the other hand, we have seen a trend leaning towards the treatment of our clients and the public in general. Further, professional standards (ethical rules) are concentrating more in the area of how the professional, or business man, or elected official treats his constituency rather than his colleague. We are also seeing increased concentration on standards that guide our work product toward a fair treatment of our public and consumers. Some of this has been forced upon us by the increase in legal action, but I like to think that most of it is the result of more caring people who wish to improve the status of themselves and their chosen profession or vocations.

Reprinted by permission of George D. Anderson.

The Evolvement of Accounting Ethics _____

The evolvement of ethics in the accounting profession has been interesting. Today in the public accounting profession there are many practices accepted which would have been considered highly innovative and unacceptable 35 or 40 years ago. Standard setting by a central body, rather than each professional interpreting the professional literature, would have been considered improper. The idea that a professional's work needed review by another professional would not have been accepted, especially when the professional to be reviewed had been in practice 20 or 30 years. Self-regulation, through quality assurance review, was unheard of and would have been considered completely unnecessary. Professionals were expected to live by certain ethical standards, and the thought that they might need to be reviewed to assure the following of those standards was out of the question. It was felt that if, by chance, there was departure from those standards, the substandard quality of the work would become obvious and the marketplace or the court would take care of it.

At that time, the CPA's main service was to perform opinion audits or to prepare unaudited statements. Tax work was an important segment of the profession, but was still considered an ancillary service in the truly professional firm. Although there were management advisory service engagements, this area or practice was not considered important, and such engagements were accepted only because of client pressures and the lack of firms or people outside the CPA profession to perform them.

The scope of practice in the last 30 or 40 years has expanded. The demand for audits and the preparation of financial statements by CPA firms has increased. The demand for opinion statements has not only expanded, but the body of technical standards that must be applied to render that opinion has grown. Also, standards are being promulgated by central bodies (the FASB and the ASB) allowing less latitude in the use of professional judgment in the application of those standards.

The Evolvement of Tax Work _____

There has been a tremendous growth in the scope and complications of tax work. The volume of literature published in the tax area has continued to grow. Whereas a tax service contained four or five volumes thirty or forty years ago, twelve or fifteen volumes are needed today.

With the advent of the computer, the management advisory service area became more important. The CPA had been the natural one to take over the area of income tax practice after the income tax law was adopted in 1913, because he understood accounting and business transactions. The same is true of the computer area when applied to the recording of business transactions and their control. The CPA, again, fills a void created by demand. As a consequence, the CPA has become the natural adviser to business and the one to aid in solving many complicated problems that need proper analysis.

Also, nationally, over the past 10 or 15 years, great changes have taken place in the social environment we live in. Many people feel there should be increased competition among members of a profession. The professions have been viewed as monopolies that work *only* for the economic good of their membership. Also, the decline in the regulatory attitude of government in all sectors of our economy has had its effect upon the professions.

Consumerism in the Accounting Profession

The rise of consumerism placed all businesses and professions including CPA's under fire. The question was asked, "Is the licensing of professions and the so-called 'ethics' restraints they adopt, a benefit to the public, or to the members of *that* profession?" Does it really serve the public interest to bar advertising, solicitation and competitive bidding? Do such bars really affect the quality of work of the professional? Or are these artificial restraints not needed; and, do they in fact, harm the public interest?

These questions were asked in court and the courts, in affect, ruled against the professions. The courts have held that licensing of the professions and the subsequent monitoring of those licensed is in the public interest, but that restraints placed by members of a profession upon themselves relating to solicitation, competitive bidding and advertising are not needed to assure the performance of quality work and, in fact, can constitute a restraint of free trade.

All of this, and subsequent actions by people in the profession, caused a great deal of concern to the leadership of the AICPA as to the retention of professional status by CPA's. Bill Gregory, as he left the chairmanship of the AICPA in 1980, warned of the steady push toward commercialism by many of the firms. He warned that the competition between small and large firms and from groups outside the profession could cause us to lose our professional status and, subsequently, our franchise.

Also, prior to this time, the CPA profession had come under attack from Senator Metcalf of Montana and from Congressman Moss of California. These individuals had berated the profession for the quality of work being performed. Although the profession took remedial action, that action was late and was not as well accepted by the profession as it should have been. As a consequence, Congressmen Dingle, Wyden and Brooks took up the cudgel and once again the profession came under fire from Washington.

But prior to Dingle, Wyden and Brooks, the Board of Directors of the AICPA, saw the necessity to look for some long range solutions to the problem. Commercialism within the profession was growing, competition was increasing and professionalism was waning. Relationships were becoming strained with our fellow professionals, among the members of our own profession, with clients and with the public in general. Perceptions were growing that business failures were really audit failures. This endangered the profession's public image. Hence, the appointment of the standards of professional conduct committee was made in 1984.

Ethical Concerns for the Future

The committee was charged with considering the changing economic, legal, social and regulatory environment and evaluating the relevance of present ethical standards to professionalism, integrity and commitment to both quality service and the public interest. The committee was further asked to consider the institute's role in the process of establishing standards of professional conduct and to recommend a course of action by the AICPA. Shortly after this charge was given to the committee, five concerns identified by the future issues committee were added. These concerns were:

1. Expansion of services and products in public practice,

2. Changes in the nature and extent of competition in the profession,

3. The role of self regulation,

4. Improving the quality of practice, and

5. Independence and objectivity.

The result of the committee's deliberations was the issuance of a report entitled "Restructuring Professional Standards to Achieve Professional Excellence in a Changing Environment." The report was the result of much research and debate and although there was a strong consensus within the committee in favor of the recommendations in the report, there were necessary compromises.

Recommendations of the Committee

The committee decided very early that changes were needed in the ethics code. It was not adequate to carry this profession into the future. In light of the competition and commercialism, it could have, in fact, carried the seeds of our destruction. There was a need for a program that would result in *educational* and *remedial* actions for the members of the profession.

The committee came to the conclusion that a new approach should be designed that would reach certain goals. That approach should:

1. Enhance the quality of work done by the CPA;

2. Address the public interest as it relates to the CPA's work;

3. Provide more guidance as to ethical behavior;

4. Emphasize compliance with broad positively-stated standards as well as behavioral rules;

5. Establish a pro-active monitoring program for firms, to aid in finding and correcting substandard work;

6. Extend the application of standards to those CPA's not in public practice; and

7. Provide guidance on responding to the changing practice environment.

As I previously stated, the committee decided that the prior code of ethics was not adequate and that there was a need for a more positively-stated code. The prior code, for instance, contained a concepts section which provided positive guidance but was not enforceable. Only the rules — the "thou shalt nots" — were enforceable. Those rules constituted the *minimum* acceptable ethical behavior expected from a CPA. Those "thou shalt nots" told us how to stay out of trouble, not how to perform at our best.

The New Code of Ethics

The new code, recommended by the committee, consists of two sections — the first, sets forth the principles of professional conduct and is presented in a positive vein. This section is based on the premise that members assume an ethical obligation when they join the AICPA. Therefore, the principles state the basic tenets of ethical and professional conduct, state the responsibilities of members to the public, clients and colleagues and give guidance as to performance of professional responsibilities. It gives guidance to all members, those in *industry, education* and *government* as well as to those in public practice. These principles are enforceable through the rules of behavior. It is still necessary to have "thou shalt nots," as positively-stated rules are virtually impossible to enforce.

Enforcement is, of necessity, voluntary. The AICPA can only rely on moral suasion to enforce its rules of conduct, they do not carry the force of law. This explains why it is important that the AICPA be looked upon as a professional organization in which membership represents a level of professional achievement greater than the mere possession of a CPA certificate. It must be a body that continually monitors and strives to improve the quality of its members' professional services.

The principles section contains an article that discusses the scope and nature of services. This is the first time this subject has been discussed in an official institute publication. This article and chapter four of the report caused some of the greatest controversy within the committee. The content was softened by subsequent actions of the implementation committee and the board of directors. However, it is a start toward determining what the profession's ethical considerations must be toward non-attest engagements. Such engagements are important to the profession and, in fact, are becoming more important. The profession must determine where this work fits within the ethical framework. Care must be taken that its importance does not completely overshadow the performance of the service CPA's are licensed to do - the attest function.

The committee next addressed the need for self-regulation and recommended that the institute should have an effective practice-monitoring program for its members. Continuing membership in the institute will be predicated upon compliance by the member firm with this quality monitoring program.

When I came into practice some 40 years ago, it would have been considered completely unnecessary for one member of the profession to review another's work. The interpretation of the accounting literature was left to the professional. This has changed along with the trend toward a narrowing of the latitude to interpret signified by the advent of the FASB and other bodies designated by council to interpret technical standards.

The committee debated extensively over the form that practice monitoring should take. Desk reviews were considered, some combinations with state boards were looked at, and even the use of outside examiners was considered. It was finally decided that field reviews, comparable to those performed by the division for firms, best filled the needs of the membership.

I am a great supporter of the quality review process. Review is the stimulation needed to bolster the motivation to keep the practice on line. All firms have the motivation to do quality work but they need stimulation to bolster that motivation.

The committee also recommended that all members should comply with a 120 hour every three (3) years CPE requirement. In addition, to become a member of the AICPA after the year 2000, the candidate must have completed an additional 30 hours of post baccalaureate work. Changes were also recommended as to how the rules of professional conduct should be enforced. Recommendations as to the handling of complaints, the composition of the joint trial board and public file maintenance are also contained within the report.

This report was submitted to council at the annual meeting in Kansas City in the fall of 1986. Council agreed that the report should be implemented and an implementation committee was appointed under the direction of Marvin Strait. That committee reported to the board of directors their recommendations for implementation. No substantive changes were made in the content of the report.

The implementation package was discussed by council at its meeting in Phoenix in May of 1987. After some spirited debate, the council accepted overwhelmingly the changes made by the implementation committee and agreed to send six propositions to the membership for vote.

The six proposals voted upon by the members in early 1987 were:

1. A new restructured code of conduct — principles and rules.

2. The practice monitoring program.

3. CPE requirement — for members in public practice —
   120 hours over a three year period.

4. CPE requirement - for members not in public practice — a
   phase-in from 60 hours at commencement to 90 hours after
   three years.

5. A requirement that after the year 2000, a candidate applying
   for membership in the AICPA must have completed 30 extra
   semester hours beyond the baccalaureate requirement.

6. Changes in trial board and enforcement procedures.

It was decided by council that the membership should vote on these six propositions separately. Each proposition required a 2/3 majority of those voting to pass. The period until November 1st was devoted to an educational and communications program. This conveyed to the membership the maximum amount of information possible relative to the proposed changes.

The result of all of this work was extremely successful and very gratifying. The six propositions voted upon all passed well above the needed two-thirds majority. The lowest percentage attained was 72% and the highest 92%. Probably most gratifying was that over 70% of the membership voted - which means that in excess of 50% of the total membership voted in favor of all of the propositions.

Since passage of the six propositions, the AICPA has proceeded with their implementation in an expeditious manner. The new code of ethics has been published and distributed to the membership. The practice monitoring program is being designed and put into action as quickly as possible. Changes are being affected in the operations of the ethics committee to comply with the new changes. The educational area of the AICPA is being strengthened in order to help schools comply with the 150 hour requirement, and to help members comply with the new CPE requirement.

While all this was taking place, the FTC instituted an investigation of the prior code of ethics. That investigation was carried on during the entire time the SPC committee met (3 1/2 years). Although the committee did not try to design their report to try and satisfy the FTC, there were recommendations made which the committee felt would help satisfy the law that has developed in the last few years relative to competition within the professions.

The main area of the code attached by the FTC was the prohibitions on contingent fees and commissions. The committee recommended in their original report that contingent fees be allowed, but that the member would be considered to have lost independence as to that client during the period of the contingent fee engagement. This recommendation was voted upon by council at their 1986 spring meeting. Placed before the membership for consideration, it lost by one vote. As a consequence, the prior prohibition against contingent fees was retained in the new code.

A recommendation for a change in the commission rule was made by the SPC committee which would have allowed commissions under circumstances approved by the senior technical committees. This recommendation was not accepted by council and again the prior complete prohibition was retained in the final draft voted upon.

At the spring Council Meeting in Boca Raton on May 19, 1988, council authorized the board of directors of the AICPA to negotiate these rules with the FTC. The resultant compromise was to be brought back to a special meeting of council in August of 1988 for discussion and approval or disapproval. This meeting was held in Chicago and a compromise developed by AICPA legal counsel was overwhelmingly adopted.

As you know, this compromise reached with the FTC will allow the acceptance of contingent fees and commissions on engagements that do not involve clients with whom independence must be maintained.

1. As to contingent fees and commissions, the order, in substance, provides:

   A. AICPA may ban contingent fees and commissions as to all attest clients for the periods of the attest engagement and of historical financial statements covered by the attest engagements.

   B. AICPA may ban *all* undisclosed commissions.

    C. AICPA is required to permit only contingent fees and fully disclosed commissions for non-attest clients.

    D. "Attest Service" means any audit or review of financial statements or compilation of a financial statement when third party use is reasonably expected and the CPA has not disclosed a lack of independence, and any examination of prospective financial information.

2. Other items covered by the order, including referral fees, solicitation, advertising and the use of trade names involve no significant change from the ethical rules as amended.

The passage and adoption of this program demonstrates that the profession is responsible and that it is capable of guiding its own destiny. Without government intervention, it will attain the goals outlined by the committee. Members are urged to follow positively-stated principles of ethical conduct. The self regulatory quality assurance program will seek out substandard work and provide those practice units with *education* and *remedial procedures* for corrective purposes. The image of the CPA will be enhanced and the public interest advanced.

The standards of professional conduct in accounting are of extreme importance. If we desire to retain the profession and to improve its status, we must consider our standards the minimum acceptable behavior for a CPA. We must keep in mind the necessity to place the public interest above our own economic interests if we wish to retain the name certified *public* accountants. Many of our sister professions and businesses are being criticized for their inability to live up to standards of conduct that advance the public interest.

A couple of years ago, the Harris Poll conducted a survey. The results were gratifying but they are also scary. To live up to the reputation we enjoy according to the poll, necessitates going much beyond "minimum" standards of behavior. There must be a constant striving to improve those standards and to demonstrate that the designation, "CPA" does carry with it a desire and dedication toward excellence in professional conduct. Our profession will continue to expand because it is an important one. There is and will continue to be a high degree of reliance upon our work. We must do everything possible to deserve and retain that reliance.

This can be accomplished only if we are willing to continue to strengthen our standards and to monitor our own profession. Failure to do so will result in a loss of confidence by the public and a resultant loss in professional status. We must be willing to give up personal gain in order to increase the status of our profession as a whole.

National CPA Certificate _____

A different but related issue deals with the development of a national CPA certificate to possibly strengthen the profession. At the present time, there are 54 separate jurisdictions that may issue CPA certificates. There is only one national uniform requirement to obtain the certificate and that is passage of the uniform CPA examination. All other prerequisites are determined by the issuing jurisdictions, whose requirements run the gamut from very lenient to very strict. The model accountancy bill supported by NASBA and the AICPA is a help toward uniformity, but state legislatures, being what they are, never pass the bill without making changes.

Although I am supportive of a national certificate, I would not like to see that certificate issued by the federal government nor an agency thereof. We have been able to avoid federal control to this point and, hopefully, the profession will continue to do so in the future.

I suggest that a national, uniform certificate could be issued by the AICPA which could be recognized in all 54 jurisdictions. At the present time, the AICPA prepares and grades the examination. In conjunction with NASBA, an agency exists which actually administers the giving of the exam in certain jurisdictions on a contract basis. Of course, the jurisdiction in which the exam is given actually issues the certificate.

Would it be possible for the AICPA to determine the qualification of candidates for the examination, prepare the examination, administer the taking of the examination, grade it and, finally, issue a certificate to the successful candidates? Doing so would assure that the qualifications to obtain the certificate were uniform throughout the 54 jurisdictions as the certification would then be issued by the AICPA.

If the candidates wished to practice or hold out to be a CPA in a particular jurisdiction, it would be up to that jurisdiction's board of accountancy to determine the qualifications for licensing to practice or to hold out. The candidate would submit his certificate from the AICPA as proof of having met the educational and other requirements to sit for the exam and as proof of passing the examination. The jurisdiction in which the CPA wishes to practice or hold out as a CPA would then determine what further prerequisite should be imposed to issue a license in that jurisdiction. They could impose residence requirements (where applicable), experience requirements, continuing educational requirements, and others they might feel necessary, to meet the requirements to practice or to hold out in their jurisdiction.

The advantages of such a system are obvious. It would cause uniformity in qualifying to sit for the examination, especially in the area of education. It would also bring much more uniformity to the monitoring of professional standards and would alleviate jurisdictional problems.

There are many problems and hurdles that must be surmounted before such a program could be instituted. It would take a great deal of study and time to design and work out the problems that might arise. It took nearly fifty years to get the uniform exam accepted in all jurisdictions. Therefore, it might take considerable time to get a program such as this accepted. I think it would be worthwhile.

What I have suggested sounds difficult and somewhat revolutionary. What this profession has accomplished in the past, however, has been no less revolutionary. I have not covered the plan in detail and certainly that would be necessary to identify the pitfalls and the problems. It is not an easy concept to understand nor accept, but it could be a positive force in solving many of the professional problems as to jurisdictional differences and uniformity in the treatment of CPAs.

This is a peculiar profession. We are much more interested in raising standards of performance than in protecting our "turf" through legal action. We worry about standards of professionalism and the degradation that commercialism brings. We know we must compete because the economic strength of the world lies in competition, but we want that competition based on quality, not price.

The future of the profession is bright because of the many dedicated individuals it contains. There will always be a need and a place for the profession in the private sector, in government and in large and small practices. The need for confidence in the CPA by the business community is greater today than ever before. That need will continue to grow in the future. We must do everything possible to enhance and maintain that confidence.

Questions

1. What problems could commercialism create within the accounting profession?
2. Was there really a need for the development of a professional conduct committee? What created this need and has it been resolved?
3. Is it really necessary that we have quality reviews? Shouldn't accounting professionals be allowed to interpret standards as they feel appropriate?
4. What is the the FTC's position on commissions? Why has this position been taken?
5. What is the accounting profession's current reputation regarding ethics? What must we do to preserve this reputation?

5
Ethical Issues in the Practice of Auditing

L. GLENN PERRY

Mr. Perry is a graduate of Old Dominion University and is licensed to practice as a Certified Public Accountant in various states. He is currently a partner in Peat Marwick's Executive Office in New York. Mr. Perry was the chief accountant of the Securities and Exchange Commission's Division of Enforcement, where he was primarily responsible for the commission's financial fraud program.

Introduction

Why is everybody talking about ethics these days? Why did John Shadd, the former Chairman of the SEC donate $20 million to Harvard University to establish an ethics program? Why did the business roundtable, headed by the chairman of Citicorp orchestrate a landmark study on how big business deals with ethics? Why did the Treadway Commission or the National Commission on Fraudulent Financial Reporting deal with ethical issues? And finally, why am I writing about ethics right now?

The answer is, there is a major problem in this area and it has been especially true on Wall Street. Consider just a few of the cases. There is the pending settlement with Drexel/Burnham, the Boesky case, the Levine case, but worst of all, the Yuppie Five. Take note of this list—all young professionals. Michael David is a former associate with a major law firm in New York. Robert Salsbury is an executive with Drexel Burnham. Andrew Solomon is with a major specialist firm in Wall Street. Martin Shapiro is a stock broker with another major firm. Daniel Silverman is a customer of Shapiro. Why did these individuals, who were so successful on Wall Street, engage in insider trading? The answer is clear — it is greed. They were envious of the wealth of older professionals who earn their money the old-fashioned way.

Auditors, however, have the highest ethics of any profession. Independence and ethics are the cornerstone of the profession. If the

---

Reprinted by permission of L. Glenn Perry.

public did not have confidence in the opinions issued by auditors, then the profession would not exist. The auditing profession has the strictest rules in this area, including rules on stock ownership. Consider family relationships, for example. The father of an auditor cannot be the chairman of a company that he is auditing. Certain business relationships are also prohibited. You can only have a loan from a bank. You cannot have a loan from a commercial company and that loan has to be secured or it has to be less than ten percent of your net worth if the bank is a client. Of course, there are rules with respect to the receipt of gifts from clients, and last but not least, confidentiality requirements. For example, there are rules on the use of information in insider trading. I don't think an auditor of a client has ever been convicted of insider trading or charged.

Then, there are other confidential issues. For example, you audit both a bank and a borrower from that bank and you know that the borrower is in very poor financial condition but you can't tell the bank client until the published report gets to the bank client. More importantly, perhaps, these rules are strictly enforced by many groups.

The AICPA ethics committee constantly reviews cases, sends members to the trial board and prescribes a punishment, if necessary. The SEC strictly enforces its own independence rules which are more strict than the AICPA. The various states working through the American Institute of C.P.A.s enforce their ethical rules. And of course, private litigation also has the effect of enforcing its own ethics.

However, there will always be a few problems, both with auditors and with other groups. In one case, Jose Gomez, a partner with Grant Thornton in their Fort Lauderdale office, took a $200,000 bribe from his client, ESM Securities, and turned his head the other way knowing that a fraud was occurring. He is now in prison for twelve years. He was permanently enjoined from practicing before the SEC. But the auditors are not alone. Hertz Rent-a-Car charged customers $13 million for repairs and the customers thought they were reimbursing Hertz for the actual cost when, in fact, they were paying retail for the repairs and Hertz was having the repairs done at a discount.

There was also a recent SEC action with respect to Shearson Lehman, and one of their investors, a seventy-year old widow. A broker invested $100,000 of her insurance proceeds from the death of her son. The broker engaged in massive churning — that is purchasing and selling various stocks — and in thirteen months, he charged her $53,000 plus in commissions.

In every discipline it can be said that ethical problems exist. Nevertheless, auditors must have the highest ethics of any group because integrity of financial information is critical to the functioning of our capital in credit markets. The role of the auditor is important to the credibility of this information by the public in general, and the investors in particular.

There is another ethical issue to be addressed. The client is responsible first and foremost for the integrity of financial information. But what if the client does not properly assume that responsibility? Does the auditor then have a duty to blow the whistle in some manner? The answer is often yes. Consider a few examples.

In management's discussion and analysis, a company might say that the reason sales increased was because of volume and not price. However, the auditor knows that is not the case. So what is his responsibility? Because he is associated with the data of the annual report to shareholders, he would have to first tell his client that he would take exception to that in his report. In other words, he would disclose in his opinion, that the representation isn't true. If the client management then refused to correct the information, he would then have an obligation to go to the board of directors and report the matter. Assuming they didn't do anything, which I find to be incredible that they wouldn't, he would have the responsibility to disclose that fact in a separate paragraph of his accountant's report. Obviously, not many companies would take it that far.

In a major case a few years ago, Mattel did not disclose that it had lost one of its major customers and that its sales would be significantly reduced in the upcoming year. The SEC brought an enforcement action against Mattel for that sole fact. That is the only thing they did wrong.

The Impact of Unethical Behavior ——————————————

What is the impact of financial fraud and unethical behavior on businesses and auditors? First, there is the financial harm to investors and creditors — disillusionment with the financial system and markets and impairment of auditor credibility. What causes financial fraud and unethical behavior? Is it financial pressures that people have to deal with? In its civil injunctive against A.M. International, the SEC said the following, "During the course of the 1980 fiscal year, AM's financial position deteriorated and its management applied increasing pressure on the divisions to meet performance goals. Such pressure consisted of, among other means, threatened dismissals, actual dismissals, and character attacks on certain of the division's senior management. This pressure was in turn applied by the division's senior management to middle management. In response to the pressure, various divisions of AM engaged in widespread and pervasive accounting irregularities in order to present results of operations which conformed to budgeted performance objectives."

On another occasion, I had the responsibility of taking the testimony of one divisional controller at the SEC in Washington. He was a young C.P.A., a nice looking guy. He'd been in to confess that he had cooked the books, he had fudged the inventory numbers. During a break I asked him, "Why did you do that?"

He said, "Well, I've got a mortgage, a wife and a car payment and I had to keep my job. Simple." It is commonly the financial pressures which inspire dishonesty.

We often see more unethical conduct when compensation of management is tied to net income or performance goals, or when there is a downturn in the business environment. What is the auditor's responsibility for the detection of fraud? The public perception, generally, is that auditors should detect all fraud. They believe that the top priority of an audit is to detect fraud. They often think that business failures equal audit failures.

I think it is important for a moment to turn to the Washington scene, Congressmen Dingle has conducted hearings for a number of years, with some really profound results. Professor Briloff, a well-known professor of accounting, testified "GAAS plus GAAP equals crap." He also testified, "Financial statements are like bikinis. What they reveal is interesting, but what they conceal is critical." We then heard testimony to the effect that restatements of financial statements equal audit failures. We heard that auditors are expected to detect all fraud, auditors are failing to fulfill their role as a public watchdog, and auditors are not alerting users of financial statements of imminent business failures.

Give thought, for a moment, to some real life cases involving companies, financial fraud and the role of the auditors. Flight Transportation is a company out of Chicago. They were going public for the first time and their financial statements showed plenty of cash, airplanes, and revenues from the operations of those flights. Unfortunately, the cash didn't exist, the planes didn't exist and the revenues didn't exist. They were totally fictitious. Not surprisingly, the audit was conducted by a firm that is no longer in existence, Fox and Company, a second tier firm. In this case, Fox did nothing unethical, they just didn't comply with generally accepted auditing standards and they were enjoined by the SEC for not doing so.

Stoffer Chemical was another instance of a company which was having a bad year, and took some unethical measures to compound the problem. It went from eight LIFO pools to 280 LIFO puddles. Why might they do that? Well, if you have more puddles, if you will, it is easier to manipulate the inventory causing LIFO liquidations to produce income. But that wasn't good enough. They normally shipped goods in the first quarter because their chemicals were used in the growing season in the spring. But this particular year, they shipped the goods that would have been shipped in the first quarter in the fourth quarter and they recorded sales. That wasn't good enough, either. They shipped goods to foreign subsidiaries, who were on FIFO, not LIFO, which caused more sales to be recorded, and resulted in more LIFO liquidations in the U.S. and therefore more income. They forgot to eliminate the effects in consolidation. The commission carefully looked at their conduct in this case and concluded, not only were they ethical, but they had not violated GAAS.

Then we have Saxon Industries. Saxon was falling upon tough times and they responded in a number of ways. They wrote a computer program that would add a few items of inventory here, there and everywhere throughout the inventory. So when the auditors went out to count the inventory and check on the accuracy of the perpetual inventory, about the worst thing they found was, a discrepancy of two or three items. But they didn't realize that these small errors were everywhere. In that case, because of a number of problems, an enforcement action was brought against Fox and Company. They were enjoined by the SEC, not because they were unethical and not because they knowingly did anything wrong, but because they did not comply with GAAS.

Audit Responsibility versus Public Perception _____

The bottom line is that the public must be educated by the accounting profession concerning what the accountant's responsibilities and duties are. There is a perception that auditors look at every transaction. That is not the case. In 1988, the American Institute of Certified Public Accountants issued ten SAS's, (statements on auditing standards) for the purpose of narrowing the expectation gap between what the public perceived as the auditor's responsibility and what their real responsibilities are. Unfortunately, if anything, the gap got larger because the responsibilities of the auditors, for example, were increased concerning their obligation to detect fraud. It used to be 'nothing came to my attention' and now you have a 'positive obligation to detect fraud.' The auditing standards, themselves, have not changed. Only the rules have changed.

Consider a few examples. GAAS does not require auditors to ascertain whether the documents they examine are genuine. It doesn't issue a report saying everything they looked at was legitimate. Forgery can cause false documents to be created. There can be collusion with customers. Let me offer an example that occurred while I was at the SEC. A company was having a bad year. So, one of the salesmen says to a customer, "Joe, do me a favor. Take this product. I'm going to invoice you for it but you don't have to pay me until you sell it. In fact, you can send it back later and get full credit." Joe then says to the salesman, "Fine. Give me a piece of paper that says — a) I don't have to pay you unless I sell it, and b) I can return it for full credit, because if you get run over by a truck, I might have a problem." So they agree and the invoice was sent. Later, the auditors sent a confirmation and the confirmation came back signed by the customer saying, "Yes, I owe the money." That is pretty tough for an auditor to detect.

Regulation of Auditors

As mentioned earlier, various forms of regulation work collectively to protect the public from unprofessional and illegal conduct by auditors. Specifically, we have regulation by state licensing authorities and self-regulation within the profession itself. We have peer regulation and private litigation that is very significant within the overall context. We have federal government oversight and we have federal government enforcement. State licensing authorities also establish the entrance requirements for CPAs. They set the education requirements. They require on-the-job training before they can be certified and they often have continuing education requirements. Most important, they have the authority to revoke or suspend an auditor's license for misconduct. The SEC, for example, can prohibit an auditor from practicing before the commission. It can't do any more than that. The AICPA can expel a member but that has no real effect either. It has no effect on his practicing. Therefore, the power of the various states is a very important regulatory tool.

Among the many forms of regulation, self-review is perhaps the most important. It's almost an individual regulation — a state of mind. The fear of peer regulation. If you do something wrong, there is substantial damage to one's reputation. There is always the fear of private litigation. There is always the fear of an SEC enforcement action. All of these aspects of self-review affect or influence an individual's ethics. There are in-house quality control systems — policies and procedures concerning hiring, concerning independence. For example, every year all of the people in our firm have to sign a lengthy affidavit concerning independence and ethical issues. The affidavits are then sent to our national office where they are accumulated and all exceptions are dealt with in a very short period of time. There is extensive supervision, training, and performance appraisals of individuals. There is also an evaluation of perspective new clients. In other words, we want to avoid dealing with management teams who have poor ethics.

In addition, monitoring mechanisms exist within the in-house quality control systems. There is the review and approval of work papers and the independent preissuance reviews of financial statements. We always take disciplinary procedures for non-compliance.

If our code of ethics is violated, a punishment will result. We cannot have those types of people in our firm. Of course, there is leadership by example. Getting back to the environment that was mentioned earlier, senior management of accounting firms must demonstrate their commitment to ethics and professionalism through their actions on a day-to-day basis.

Peer Regulation

Next there is peer regulation. Basically, this is the AICPA/SEC practice section that was established in 1977 requiring that firms go through a review of their quality control procedures and compliance therewith every several years. This is performed by another firm and it has been extremely effective. One reason is due to improved quality controls. The people in firms are very mindful that a peer review is going to take place and they are concerned about the procedure. Therefore, they feel a certain amount of pressure to do a better job.

Private Litigation

Finally, private litigation is another regulatory tool. The threat of litigation is real and it is powerful. In fact, in my firm, I often say it's too real and it's too powerful. There is not only the cost of the litigation and the possible loss of monies, but there is also substantial defense costs, considerable consummation of time of the people in the firm, damage to professional reputation leading to the possible loss of clients, and the loss of opportunities to gain new clients. Auditors typically are sued whether they've done anything wrong or not. If there has been a business failure or major restatement of financial statements, I usually wonder whether we will be sued within one day, two days, or three. But I know it won't be long and I know that the plaintiffs don't know anything about what happened. Nevertheless, we will likely receive a piece of paper saying we've been sued for not complying with GAAS and GAAP. They don't know why yet or what we didn't comply with, but they're sure it was something.

Now, consider federal government oversight. The SEC has the absolute authority under the law to prescribe accounting principles. Right now the SEC relies primarily on FASB, but it has the absolute authority to override those standards of the FASB or not to follow them at all. It also has authority over the SEC practice section, the group that oversees the peer review process and evaluates the effectiveness of the public oversight board.

Another factor affecting the ethics of auditors is federal government enforcement. The FCC's division of enforcement, which conducts financial fraud investigations, in every case will take a look at the conduct of the auditor. If it believes that the auditor did not conduct himself ethically, or didn't comply with GAAS or GAAP, it will bring an enforcement action. It has the authority to enjoin the auditor and to permanently bar a CPA from further practice before the commission.

One thing that was clear to me when I was at the SEC was that firms who are members of the SEC practice section and who are peer reviewed, typically have much better quality control systems than those who are not members and therefore do not go through the peer review process. Such systems are essential because ethical problems are unavoidable.

Individuals sometimes yield to client pressures to bend rules, thereby placing business considerations above ethical and professional considerations. People who audit by conversation — and this is one of the biggest problems that I used to see when I was at the SEC — do not gather sufficient evidence to support the assertion of the client. Lack of necessary training and experience is another "people" problem.

Are auditors faced with making decisions regarding ethical behavior? Yes, all the time. Not only on their part but on the part of their clients. Overall the profession is doing a good job in seeing that auditors make the proper ethical decisions. Does the auditing profession need some help in coping with unethical behavior? Again, the answer is obviously yes. Much has been done, much has been said, and as a result, many companies are creating codes of conduct. Unfortunately, although they are trying to create a better environment, there will always be those people who are forced by financial pressures into the commission of fraud.

Questions

1. Why is the auditing profession regarded as having the highest ethics of any profession?
2. What pressures have resulted in dishonesty among accountants?
3. Does adherence to the idea, "we have not violated GAAS, GAAP, or FASB", always result in ethical behavior?
4. What are some of the current "people" problems which are plaguing the accounting profession?

6
Ethical Issues in the Practice of Auditing — A Case

DR. LARRY DEPPE

Dr. Deppe received his doctoral degree in Accounting from the University of Utah. He is currently an Assistant Professor in the School of Accountancy at Brigham Young University. He is a member of the AICPA, the NAA, the ICMA, and the AAA. His professional designations include the CPA in the State of Utah and the CMA.

Introduction

Megan Williams, CPA and junior partner at the Atlanta office of Burnam, Stewart, and Plunkett, sat at her desk and stared at the phone. She knew that one quick phone call could take a tremendous burden off her shoulders and save her firm from possible litigation. She picked up the phone to call Lloyd Evens, vice president of Murphy Aviation. He could put an end to the fraud once and for all. Before she had dialed the last number, she put the phone back on the receiver and sat back in her chair. No, she thought, the solution to this problem could not be that easy.

Murphy Aviation Inc. (MAI) is an audit client that Megan had brought into the firm only four years ago. She had worked hard to get this client. MAI produces sophisticated corporate jet components and has enjoyed a strong market share in this industry for almost ten years. Currently, the company's chief financial officer is concerned with cutting costs because of a recession in the industry. Megan considered MAI to be one of the firm's best clients, and it bothered her to see MAI being ripped off for thousands of dollars by another of the firm's audit clients, DataTech Inc.

DataTech is a high-tech computer firm that supplies computers and parts to manufacturing companies. DataTech supplies computer components that control the fuel injection systems in MAI's jet engines. Two weeks ago during the current year's audit engagement at

Reprinted by permission of Dr. Larry Deppe.

DataTech, Megan discovered that DataTech was charging too much for some of the equipment it sold to Murphy Aviation.

The contract between the two firms was explicit about its cost plus pricing procedure. While reviewing DataTech's invoice records, she discovered that exorbitant shipping charges were being added to the total invoice amount being billed to Murphy. When she inquired about this practice, she was told that it was not illegal and that it didn't violate DataTech's contract with Murphy in any way. In fact, she was more or less told to do her own job, which was to audit DataTech's financial records. They even went so far as to remind her about her responsibility as to the confidentiality of information.

Megan took it upon herself to find out more. She found that inflation of shipping costs was used only on shipments to Murphy and to no other DataTech customers. She reviewed DataTech's shipping documents for the last three years and was shocked to discover that the inflated shipping costs alone amounted to over $200,000 per year. This is certainly a material amount, considering the size of the two companies. Apparently, this discrepancy had not been uncovered by any of her firm's previous audit work with either of the companies.

The past two weeks have been miserable for Megan. She has never faced an ethical dilemma like this. At the Ethics University where she received her degree, her professors had warned the students that they would be faced with situations similar to this one. Only now can she appreciate the impact of not having taken the elective ethics class before graduating.

After some thought, she casually mentioned the matter to her senior at the firm. He told her to leave it alone since he felt that there was probably no breach of contract. He said, "Don't open a can of worms, Megan." She knew that sooner or later someone at MAI would discover the fraud and then where would her firm be? As far as Megan was concerned, her firm could be facing litigation unless it takes the proper action.

1. What action, if any, should Megan take with the information?

2. Should Megan override the opinion of her senior?

3. When is it appropriate, if ever, to reveal confidential information?

4. What are other ethical issues in the practice of audit?

Deppe:

What action, if any, should Megan take with the information?

Comment:

The first issue that must be dealt with in this case is the fact that Megan must thoroughly research and document the problem that she believes exists regarding the exorbitant shipping charges. There is no indication in the details of this case that Megan has carefully read the provisions of the contractual agreement between Murphy Aviation and Data Tech. Such contractual agreements typically are included in the permanent file of the audit working papers of a client.

Megan should thoroughly prepare herself and then discuss the issues with senior management of the accounting firm. Under no circumstances should Megan contact Murphy Aviation. Matters of this nature should be handled by the more experienced senior partners of the firm.

Comment:

In addition, it would be wise for Megan to read carefully the contractual agreement and note specifically any provisions regarding shipping charges. She should compare these provisions of the agreement to the information she has obtained from her review of the Data Tech invoices. All information from the invoices should be recorded in a clear and concise manner in supporting working papers.

If Megan determines that a problem exists, then she should prepare a memorandum to her senior at the firm. This issue should not have been discussed in a casual manner with her superior. She should have broached the subject only after she had thoroughly prepared herself by obtaining a clear understanding of the facts and only after preparing a clear and concise written presentation of the facts.

The importance of Megan having a complete understanding of the facts at hand cannot be overemphasized. An unfounded accusation against Data Tech of a matter such as this could have very serious consequences for all parties concerned. Such an accusation could affect the supplier-customer relationship of Murphy and Data Tech and could have serious implications for the production and financial functions of both firms. Loss of a major customer could adversely affect the financial condition at Data Tech. Loss of a major supplier also could place a financial strain on Murphy if Murphy either was unable to fulfill its contracts with its customers due to a lack of parts or was forced to purchase the parts from another supplier at a substantially higher price.

Comment:

Megan also might deal a severe blow to the accounting firm of which she is a junior partner. Should her accusation prove unfounded, both firms may decide that they wish to retain the services of a more responsible accounting firm resulting in the loss of two major revenue-producing audits. Additionally, word of the false accusation like this would spread quickly among prospective clients of the firm, and the business community as a whole resulting in perhaps irreparable damage to the firm's reputation and its ability to obtain and retain clients. Clearly, such consequences to the firm also are apt to adversely affect Megan's career as well.

Deppe:

Should Megan override the opinion of her senior?

Comment:

It is essential that Megan thoroughly document the alleged wrongdoing. She also would have been well-advised not to have discussed the matter with anyone at Data Tech. The case is not clear as to the organizational level of the individual at Data Tech who advised Megan not to pursue the matter. Certainly, if this advice came from a senior member of the management of the company, then there would be reason for some concern. Nevertheless, such concern might be mitigated by the fact that Megan may not have been in full possession of the facts concerning the matter and the Data Tech employee may have perceived that she was not fully informed. Indeed, Megan's discussion of a matter of such gravity with an employee of Data Tech, prior to the issue being addressed by the senior partners of the accounting firm, suggests that the accounting firm may be in need of more specific policies regarding how such matters are to be treated. The existence of such a policy could have eliminated any potential conflict between Megan and her senior.

Comment:

It seems unlikely that a matter of this nature should be presented to a client of the firm by a junior partner. The matter (assuming that there is substance to it) should have been considered carefully by the senior partners of the firm and a senior partner then should have approached a high-ranking member of the management of Data Tech. A matter of this nature never should be dealt with in an informal or haphazard manner by people with limited experience who have less than full information regarding the matter at issue.

The situation in this case also may suggest that the accounting firm should consider a more extensive mentoring program among senior and junior partners. Development of firm personnel extends beyond the review of working papers or evaluation of personal merit based upon the number of new clients brought to the firm by an individual. New partners may require assistance in developing the tact and insight needed to resolve potentially explosive situations occurring with clients. Interpersonal skills are as vital to a partner of a firm as are technical accounting, tax, or consulting skills.

Deppe:

When, if ever, is it appropriate to reveal confidential information?

Comment:

Much has been said to this point regarding the importance of determining first, the existence and then seriousness of the problem. The assumption will now be made that the problem Megan identified actually exists and is as serious as she believes it to be. Several issues then arise that must be considered.

Foremost among these issues is the need for the firm to involve its legal counsel in the deliberations pursuant to the ultimate resolution of the problem. Counsel should review the contractual agreement between Murphy and Data Tech to determine problems regarding the firm's legal liability in the matter and the appropriate conduct to pursue in addressing the parties to the problem. The firm could likely find itself liable as a result of the issue of confidential information.

The firm has a responsibility to its clients under Rule 301 of the Code of Professional Conduct not to disclose any confidential information obtained in the course of a professional engagement except with the consent of the client. The only situations in which confidential information can ethically be revealed are:

(1) when the auditor's responsibility to discharge professional standards is greater than that for confidentiality

(2) when a summons or subpoena is issued by a court of law demanding information relating to a client

(3) when a peer review of an accounting firm is conducted

(4) when a firm is responding to an inquiry as part of an investigation by the AICPA Ethics Division

Comment:

The accounting firm in this case is in possession of confidential information regarding Data Tech and its policy relating to shipping charges. Revealing this information to Murphy Aviation without the permission of the management of Data Tech could result in a suit by Data Tech against the accounting firm. Case law in this area suggests that the accounting firm could be subject to an adverse decision in a suit if it discloses or does not disclose the confidential information. Two major cases litigated in the early 1980s addressed the question of an accounting firm's responsibilities related to confidential information.

In *Consolidata Services, Inc. v. Alexander Grant & Company*, the accounting firm performed tax services for a payroll service company. The accounting firm recommended the payroll service firm to its clients and the payroll service reciprocated by recommending the accounting firm to its clients.

The payroll service firm eventually became insolvent and informed partners of the accounting firm of this fact in a private conference. The accounting firm (on advice of legal counsel) requested that the payroll service firm notify its customers of its insolvency. The management of the payroll services firm refused to do so and asked that the accounting firm wait ten days before informing the customers of the payroll services firm of the firm's condition in order to allow time to arrange financing to avoid the insolvency.

The partners of the accounting firm determined that they would call all twelve of their firm's clients served by the payroll services firm in order to advise these clients not to send additional payroll money to the firm. The remaining twenty-four customers of the payroll services firm were not informed of the insolvency.

The payroll services firm sued the accounting firm for breach of contract for breaking an obligation of confidentiality. The payroll services firm prevailed and was awarded $1.3 million.

The case of *Fund of Funds Limited v. Arthur Anderson & Co.* produced what ostensibly is a contradictory result to the court's finding in the *Consolidata* case. In the *Fund of Funds* case, the accounting firm audited both a mutual investment company and a natural resources company. The mutual investment company purchased from the natural resources company for $90 million more than 400 natural resource properties under an agreement stipulating that the mutual investment company would be subject to terms no less favorable than those extended to other customers of the natural resources company.

During the audit of the natural resources company, the accounting firm discovered that the mutual investment company had, in fact, paid a premium for the properties it had purchased. The accounting firm did not report this information to the management of the mutual investment company. The management of the mutual investment company did not discover that a premium had been paid until considerably later.

Upon the discovery of this information, the management of the mutual investment fund contended that the accounting firm had an obligation to inform them of the violation of the agreement or to resign from one of the audits. The accounting firm contended that it had a responsibility under the Code of Professional Conduct not to divulge the information.

The court agreed with the mutual investment company and awarded its shareholders a judgment of $80 million.

The accounting firm in the present case likely could be sued by either Data Tech if the information is divulged or by Murphy Aviation if the information is not divulged. Furthermore, the accounting firm could be viewed as having a conflict of interest as was suggested in the *Fund of Funds* case. It is clear that the area of confidential client information is fraught with danger and requires very skillful legal counsel. To suggest in advance the possible decision of a court in this matter is obviously foolhardy.

Deppe:

What other issues related to this case should be considered?

Comment:

Any suit on the part of either Data Tech or Murphy Aviation will require the accounting firm to consider the provisions of *Statement of Financial Accounting Standards No. 5, Accounting for Contingencies.* The accounting firm must ensure that appropriate disclosures regarding such suits be included in the notes to the financial statements of the client firm.

As stated earlier, further investigation of the matter may reveal that Data Tech has acted inappropriately. The accounting firm may wish to consider the effect of the overcharges on the financial statements as a whole and the need for a qualification of the auditor's report. Should the management of Data Tech require any persuasion, the threat of a qualified opinion may be sufficient motivation to persuade Data Tech's management to rectify the situation, particularly if Data Tech is a publicly-traded company subject to regulation by the Securities and Exchange Commission.

The alleged failure of other auditors in the accounting firm to discover the exorbitant charges may raise questions about the planning, supervision, and conduct of audits the firm performs. Attention should be given to these matters as well as to the qualifications of members of the professional staff if these individuals did in fact fail to make this discovery. Any weaknesses in the quality of the firm's audit practice should be corrected prior to any future peer review.

Comment:

Some questions might be raised concerning the competence of the management of Murphy Aviation if the overcharging persisted for an extended period without being observed by Murphy personnel. Questions also might be raised regarding Murphy's system of internal control and the accounting firm's evaluation and testing of this system.

Comment:

Megan should avoid the temptation to make an anonymous phone call informing Murphy of the mischief occurring. The procedures for properly dealing with the situation have already been discussed. Such a phone call could have the same disastrous results as a call from Megan in which she identifies herself. Similarly, Megan should avoid sending members of the audit staff to Murphy with instructions that these staff members audit the specific area that surely would result in the overcharges being brought to light. Megan also should avoid the temptation to go to Murphy and reveal the pricing problem without divulging the source of the information. Any attempt at dealing with this situation in a less than forthright manner could result in lawsuits, loss of clients, loss of firm reputation, and personal distress to Megan herself.

The case also suggests the need for accounting firms to consider the policy to be employed when disagreements arise between professionals in the firm. Megan, for example, may have a legitimate disagreement with her senior partner. If, after appropriate discussion, the disagreement persists, then Megan should be allowed her dissent in an appropriate manner in the working papers.

Questions

1. Since the problem described in this chapter is between the two companies, does Megan need to be concerned?
2. What are your first reactions regarding Megan's position?
3. Should Megan go higher in the firm for support? Is her senior as unethical as the company?
4. Could Megan have called the company directly if the problem was less material?
5. What could/should Megan have done to prepare herself for this situation and for others which will likely occur in the future?
6. Under what circumstances can confidential information be revealed to outside parties?
7. What legal precedents exist regarding confidentiality? Do they contain the same result? What is your opinion regarding the contradiction?

___7
Ethical Issues in the Practice of Tax___

JAMES B. DOX

Mr. Dox graduated from Northern Illinois University with a bachelor's degree in accounting and is a Certified Public Accountant in Illinois and Texas. He is currently the partner in charge of tax for the Los Angeles office of Ernst and Whinney. He has significant insurance industry experience in taxation and is a frequent speaker on such matters.

Introduction ___

Today's tax practitioner must be an agile tightrope walker, able to balance a host of divergent demands. Maintaining one's equilibrium is indeed difficult as a clamor of voices shout conflicting commands.

In one corner, you hear the client — requesting daring, aggressive moves. At the opposing end of the arena stands the Internal Revenue Service, carefully scrutinizing every step, poised to break your fall with a net of potentially painful penalties. And, somewhere in the middle, sits the Federal Tax Subcommittee of the American Institute of Certified Public Accountants, offering its guidance to help you traverse this unsteady wire.

In light of this obstacle-laden course, contemporary tax practitioners are bound to encounter ethical dilemmas as they attempt to cross this often obscure pathway. Fortunately, if one is able to keep pace with the proliferation of IRS rules and AICPA standards, many of these dilemmas can be resolved successfully. Unfortunately, this pace shows no signs of slowing, and thus tax professionals will be forced to continue watching their step in the years to come.

The AICPA Code of Professional Conduct ___

The American Institute of Certified Public Accountants (AICPA) makes a concerted effort to provide sound ethical guidelines for its members

___
Reprinted by permission of James B. Dox.

nationwide. Most recently, the organization revised its ethical rules in January of 1988.[1] Important principles and rules dealing with such issues as independence, objectivity, standards of field work and expressions of opinion — as they relate to tax preparation and tax advisory services, are addressed.

Regarding independence, the question frequently arises, "Can a CPA who provides audit services also provide tax advisory services, without sacrificing independence?" The answer is, yes. Resolving a tax doubt in favor of a client is perfectly acceptable, provided that the practitioner has a reasonable basis (e.g., appropriate research, technical competence), for arriving at that conclusion.

The issue of independence can also emerge in relation to litigation that could occur between a client and a CPA. In this regard, the general consensus is that tax-related litigation is seldom significant enough to cause an audit independence conflict. To minimize potential problems, however, it is advisable to refrain from providing additional advisory services to the litigant until the matter is resolved. Similarly, if a fee dispute occurs, a curtailment of services also might be appropriate — although such disputes typically do not impair independence.

In the area of objectivity, some perplexing situations can arise. If a practitioner has or is serving as a tax advisor, this advocacy role could result in difficulties when the auditor role is assumed, and an attest function is required. While some commentators feel this situation creates an irreconcilable conflict, as a practical matter, such conflicts can in fact be overcome. The key is in utilizing a conservative, consistent, common-sense approach in the attest function, while clearly performing in an advocacy posture once removed from the audit role.

Consider this scenario: while serving as a tax advisor, you recommend a specific strategy to your client. The strategy is aggressive, but within the bounds of fair play. As an advocate, it is your ethical responsibility to bring this strategy to your client's attention. At year end, you must switch roles, and function as an auditor. At this point, a conservative presentation of the issue might prompt a recommendation to the client that they postpone recognition of any tax benefit associated with the previously proposed strategy, until such time as the IRS has had an opportunity to pass judgment on it. This is certainly an acceptable approach. To avoid any client-relation problems early on, it is advisable to discuss the financial statement presentation with your client at the same time you are exploring a particular tax strategy.

Regarding field work, the established standards in this area — which are generally associated with audit-related activities — are equally applicable to tax preparation. Specifically, these standards

---

[1]American Institute of certified Public Accountants, *Professional Ethics for Certified Public Accounts*, New York, N.Y., 1988.

include professional competence, professional care, planning, supervision, and the use of relative data to support conclusions.

In terms of expressing an opinion, the general public is often confused regarding the role of a CPA as a tax practitioner, versus as an audit participant. There is a clear distinction between the opinion signature on an audit report, and the signing of a tax return as the "preparer". This latter signature indicates that the CPA has examined the tax return and accompanying schedules, and to the best of the individual's knowledge, the information is true and complete. The examination of all underlying data is not a prerequisite to tax return signing, and there should be no inference that an attest function has been fulfilled.

In addition to the AICPA's general guidelines, the organization's Federal Tax Subcommittee issued revised standards in August of 1988.[2] Formally titled, "Statements On Responsibility In Tax Practice", there are eight statements in all. These most recent revisions are seen in part as a response to the now dormant Treasury Department Circular 230 amendments (1986), as well as a reaction to the introduction of the substantial understatement penalty via the 1982 tax legislation.

Of the eight statements, numbers one and eight are of particular importance to tax preparers. Statement number one introduces a new standard — the "realistic possibility standard". This standard suggests that tax preparers cannot recommend taking a position on a return unless they have a good faith belief that the issue, if challenged, has a realistic possibility of succeeding on its merits in a judicial or administrative setting. This standard is viewed as being much tighter than the reasonable basis standard, however, it is considered less stringent than the substantial authority rule. In a similar vein, these statements advise the CPA not to prepare a return, or to sign as a return preparer, in situations that take a position that violates the "realistic possibility" standard. In fulfilling this standard, the CPA can rely not only on the section 6661 authority sources, but also on "non-precedential authority" such as well-reasoned tax articles, treaties, and IRS letter rulings.

These statements further delineate that a CPA can recommend a position that is not "frivolous", and does not meet the realistic possibility standard, if there is disclosure on the return. In other words, if your position falls between frivolous and realistic possibility, disclosure is required; if the position exceeds the realistic possibility standard, disclosure is not required.

These statements are clearly more stringent than the old "reasonable basis" standard. Over the years, in fact, the reasonable basis standard eroded significantly to the point where it was dubbed the

---

[2]These statements revise and supersede a series of statements issued between 1964 and 1977.

"laugh-aloud" test. In other words, if after examination of the issue and associated research, your conclusion didn't cause you to start laughing, the item was considered to have passed the reasonable basis standard.

Statements number one and eight contain two other important provisions. Specifically, a CPA, when appropriate, should advise a client as to the potential penalty consequences of a recommended tax position, and the opportunity — if any, to avoid such penalties through disclosure. Additionally, preparers are advised to not recommend positions that exploit the audit selection process, or serve as mere arguing positions to secure leverage in the bargaining process of a settlement negotiation.

Preparers should also be aware of Statement number five. This statement addresses the issue of whether a CPA can recommend a tax return position that departs from the treatment accorded an item in an administrative proceeding or court decision, with respect to a prior tax return. Unless the taxpayer is bound to a specified treatment in the later year, such as by a formal closing agreement, this statement contends that the CPA is not restricted from recommending a more advantageous tax treatment for a later year's return.

Tax preparers should similarly be cognizant of Statement number six. This Statement explores the situation in which a CPA becomes aware of an error in a client's previously-filed tax return, or of a client's failure to file a required tax return. In these instances, the CPA is obligated to inform the client of the error, and to recommend appropriate reparatory action. These recommendations may be given orally, and the CPA is not mandated to inform the IRS.

Circular 230 — The Tax Practitioners' Bible

While the AICPA's Federal Tax Subcommittee's guidelines are unquestionably recommended reading, the Treasury Department's Circular 230 is nothing short of required reading. If tax practitioners run afoul of the behavior rules contained within Circular 230, they may well pay a personal price — both monetarily, and in terms of severe professional restrictions.

The guiding standard in Circular 230 is called "due diligence" — a standard that is relatively loosely defined. Due diligence applies to: preparing or assisting in the preparation of returns, oral or written representations and submissions to the IRS on behalf of clients, and, providing, oral and written representations to clients relative to tax matters. If the due diligence standard is not met, the violating practitioner can be required to appear before the IRS Director of Practice to explain the indiscretion. Possible consequences include the practitioner, as well as the practitioner's firm, being temporarily suspended from practicing before the IRS. Or, if the violation is deemed serious enough, disbarment.

Penalties

Penalties have indeed become an IRS hallmark. In fact, since 1954, the number of established penalties has risen from 13 to some 150. Realizing that this penalty proliferation may well be unmanageable, former IRS Commissioner Biggs sponsored a penalty study late last year. In February of 1989, a report was submitted to the House Ways And Means Subcommittee on 'Oversight'. Based on this report, legislative action is anticipated in the near future.[3]

The report contained several recommendations regarding new standards of behavior for tax practitioners. The reasonable basis standard, for example, would be replaced by "reasonable care" — a standard that is seen as stronger and more well-defined. The report also recommended that the normative standard for issues of tax law is "substantial authority". The definition of substantial authority would be expanded to include non-precedential authority.

In relation to the issue of frivolous positions, the IRS framed its recommendation in the form of a commentary. Essentially, the commentary indicated that a tax practitioner would not be permitted to participate in any position that was deemed frivolous, even if disclosure was provided.

In an effort to bring some semblance of manageability to the penalty process, the IRS report included a recommendation to establish a simple three-tiered penalty system. If reasonable care was not exercised or disclosure was not present, the first tier imposes a 20 percent penalty. The second tier, a penalty of 50% applies if one claimed a frivolous position. The third tier, a 100 percent penalty, would be applied when fraud was determined to exist.

Considering that the current 150 penalties generate significant tax revenue, it is certainly debatable whether these proposals — which admittedly would reduce the Treasury's intake — can withstand the current budget crisis.

A Look Toward The Future ————————————————————

Regardless of what specific regulations are adopted, it is clear that more and more tax return disclosure will be required. This trend toward increased disclosure may well collide head-on with another rising issue, that of contingent fees. Inherently, contingent fees invite more aggressive tax transactions, and ethical conflicts are bound to emerge.

Many firms are also becoming increasingly involved in non-traditional areas, such as benefit consulting and valuation. In the

---

[3]"Improved Penalty Administration and Compliance Tax Act" (HR 2528) was introduced on June 1, 1989.

coming years, navigating these unchartered waters will likely produce a wave of ethical challenges.

Compounding these future challenges is the fact that the IRS continues to pressure tax professionals to become their extension — to be both practitioner and regulator — dual roles that are indeed difficult to combine.

Survival Today

Clearly, contemporary tax practitioners are faced with a myriad of conflicting demands, as well as with a plethora of IRS penalties. Where these factors intersect, ethical dilemmas are bound to emerge.

When the inevitable occurs, a key weapon for survival is communication. Don't try to solve problems in isolation. Turn to your colleagues for advice — talk to practitioners outside your firm. Find out how others have dealt with similar issues.

Communication provides a safety net — a net that is essential equipment for today's tightrope-walking tax professional.

Also, constantly challenge the limits of your tax consulting strategies. Some clients are more than willing to stretch to the "edge of the envelope," and then step back a reasonable distance when challenged. On the other hand, the "card laid is a card played" client posture will definitely create a more conservative tax consulting position. In this regard, the CPA must know the client's attitude and demeanor, so as to avoid difficult ethical dilemmas.

And, finally, a client who clearly gets too aggressive for the CPA's comfort level will create perhaps the greatest challenge of all. Fees generated under these circumstances seldom support the monetary cost or mental anguish of defending ethical challenges that surface in violations of professional standards, or Treasury practice rules. The CPA must have an acceptable comfort level with both the strategy, and the client response, before recommending the tax planning opportunity.

Questions

1. What is the "tight-rope" dilemma which tax practitioners are faced with? Why has it occurred?
2. What kind of a position must an individual take when he or she is involved in both the tax and the audit functions for a company/ Is this a valid possibility?
3. What are the standards which are entitled "Statements on Responsibility in Tax Practice"?
4. What is meant by the phrase, "due diligence"?

5. What is the three-tiered penalty system imposed by the IRS?
6. What is the conflict between increased disclosure and contingency fees?
7. What are some suggested ideas for solving ethical concerns in the tax profession?

____8
Ethical Issues in the Practice of Tax — A Case ____

DR. DAVID N. STEWART

Dr. Stewart is currently a Professor in the School of Accountancy at Brigham Young University. He received his doctoral degree from the University of Florida. He is a member of the AICPA, the Utah Association of CPA's, the ATA, and the AAA. He has written several articles relating to tax applications.

Introduction _____

A good friend, Kevin Dumars, is sitting in your office. Kevin is a self-employed CPA who specializes in tax-related services as well as some write-up work and consulting. Kevin is very distraught and has come to you for some advice on what he should do relative to a tax engagement on which he is currently working.

Kevin explains that one of his clients, Joe Grindwald, recently brought in his financial information for the preparation of his 1988 personal income tax returns. Joe and his spouse are a retired couple who basically live off their social security payments and some modest investment income. However, they do have a sizeable Individual Retirement Account (IRA), and they are planning to start receiving annual distributions from their IRA to ease some of their financial pressures. The IRA along with a small home, represents the majority of their net worth.

Joe and his wife have not had to pay any significant income taxes for a number of years and according to Kevin's projections will not have to pay any significant taxes in the future. However, Kevin was concerned when he discovered a Form 1099-R in Joe's financial information which reported a lump-sum distribution to Joe of $560,000. This amount represents Joe's entire IRA. When Kevin asked Mr. Grindwald about the distribution, Joe explained that he had not received a lump-sum distribution, but that his investment counselor, Randy Gregory, had merely shifted the funds into a "better" investment.

_____
Reprinted by permission of Dr. David N. Stewart.

Kevin has contacted Randy and discovered that based on advice from the investment firm's tax counsel, Randy had distributed the entire IRA so that Joe could take advantage of some income averaging provisions that would phase out after 1988. However, when Kevin checked out the rules pertaining to lump-sum distributions, he discovered the following:

1. Even if Joe is eligible for the special income averaging rules, Joe's overall tax would be close to 25 percent of the IRA amount (or about $140,000).

2. However, the more Kevin had researched the lump-sum distribution rules, the more he discovered that Joe is not even eligible for the averaging rules and his real tax liability (including penalties for excess distributions) will represent almost 50 percent of the IRA (or $280,000).

Kevin is obviously concerned because he knows that if he tells Joe that he owes $280,000 in taxes, Joe will be totally devastated. Joe has recently been informed that if he doesn't have some fairly extensive and potentially dangerous surgery, he will shortly be blind. Therefore, his mental and emotional state is shaky at best.

The Problem _____

Earlier this morning, Kevin has been in contact with Randy and has explained what the tax consequences are to the lump-sum distribution. Randy assures Kevin that Kevin's conclusions must be in error and that Randy will check with his own tax counsel. Later that morning, Kevin returns to the office and finds a message from Randy. The message states that the 1099-R has been issued in error. In fact, the $560,000 was never distributed according to Randy and their records would be "adjusted" to show that fact.

Kevin is elated to receive the message because now Joe's tax liability will be minimal. However, Kevin is uncomfortable because he knows that in fact the lump-sum distribution was made on their advice and that when the consequences were called to their attention (with the accompanying potential legal liability), they miraculously discovered a bookkeeping error that solved the problem.

Kevin has come to you for advice on what to do in this situation. He is not the one who is changing records or backdating transactions. However, he knows that is what is happening. On the other hand, if he files the tax return as originally computed, it would financially and emotionally devastate the Grindwalds.

1. What is your advice to Kevin?

2. If you accept Randy's statements, are you being an advocate for your client or are you committing tax preparer fraud?

3. What are other ethical issues in the practice of tax?

Discussion

Stewart:

The CPA in this case was fairly surprised when the client had a 1099-R indicating the existence of a $560,000 distribution. The initial assumption was that the investment people were probably just rolling this over from one IRA to another, and all that they would be doing is reporting it and backing it out again. Thus, there would be no real tax consequence.

However, according to Kevin's research, the client was not eligible for any special provisions and, in fact, because it was such a large distribution, additional penalties and taxes would be assessed. As a result, nearly 50 percent of the entire IRA would be owed to the government.

To make matters worse, the CPA was fairly close to this couple (as is commonly the case) and he happened to know that this gentleman was going in for some surgery. There was a good chance that if it wasn't successful, he would lose his eyesight. The client was under a fair amount of stress. Kevin was somewhat hesitant to go to him and tell him that basically half of his net worth was owed in tax.

What would you ethically do at this particular point if you were that CPA? Would you simply report the truth and pay the tax liability of $280,000? What options are available to the CPA?

Comment:

I would call the taxpayer in and say you've got a 1099 issued by this company, and it doesn't agree with what you're telling me. The investment company is telling me that there was no taxable transaction at all. However, they've now sent you a 1099. I am advising you to talk to them and find out what's going on. The responsibility lies with Randy and that's where further questions should be directed.

Comment:

I would go back to the present investment counselor before I even contacted the taxpayer to make sure that they did what they had claimed or what appears to be done. In other words, I would have gone back to the professional financial counselor that has done this and make sure that I haven't missed anything.

Comment:

There's a more pragmatic problem here. Who's going to pay the CPA's fees for doing all the research? In the past, this has been a standard, rather routine return and the client hasn't ever paid much. That becomes a real issue. Are you going to run up a big bill to the taxpayers without them knowing that you have a potential problem? What would I do? I would contact the clients before I did all the research and suggest to them that there is a possible problem and a potential for the fees to be significantly different than what they were anticipating. I don't believe you should go forward without some communication with the client that there was additional work that was being done. There's nothing in the case here to suggest that there is an engagement letter that specifies any additional services or anything other than just a simple tax return. I think that could be a real issue or dispute between the client and the practitioner if there's not some communication.

Stewart:

It's important that the CPA not make this his problem. By doing what is suggested here, he has made it his problem. And if he goes back to his client and talks about the fee, talks about what Randy's advice was, and talks about getting some additional facts, he's made it his problem. I don't think he ought to make it his problem.

In fact, let me read something more into the paragraph. It says earlier that Kevin contacts Randy and explains what he thinks the tax consequences are to Randy. And Randy says, "Are you sure? That's got to be a mistake. This is a fairly large investment firm. We wouldn't make that kind of a mistake, but I will certainly check into it." Kevin goes one step further and suggests that, and this is the part that perhaps was unethical, maybe there was a mistake made. Maybe there wasn't a distribution.

Perhaps Kevin plants the seed in Randy's mind. Because if there truly was a distribution then somebody, namely the investment firm, might have a potential liability. It would then seem like some real strange advice was given. And, sure enough, in checking into it, Randy magically finds a bookkeeping error. With a corrected 1099, a distribution was never made. That's what was told to the CPA. This is good news to Kevin because that gets him off the hook. Now, he can simply file a return as if there was no income from the IRA.

However, the key is that Kevin knows certainly that the distribution was made. All that ever took place was a paper transaction. No money ever went anywhere. The account had gone out from an IRA to another investment account that was no longer technically in that individual retirement account and should then been taxed as a distribution. As one gentleman explained, it's like playing chess. If you haven't taken your hand off the piece you can still change your mind. And that's exactly what happened. But, what are the ethical implications?

Comment:

I'm a little alarmed. Kevin explains that one of his clients, Joe Grindwald, recently brought in his financial information for the preparation of his 1988 personal income tax returns. He found this lump sum distribution which is more than the IRA. He couldn't accumulate that much at $2,000 a year. Therefore, it must have been a profit sharing plan, based more or less on income. So apparently the client has had some good income in addition to his social security. He's got to start drawing at 70-1/2. If you take 70-1/2 into that amount of money, he is going to pay taxes.

As a result, the client should have known that he was making fairly good money before and thus, he wouldn't have that IRA. He knew this problem was building up.

Comment:

One of the questions we really struggle with in taxes is — a t what point in time do I call my client a liar? In other words, he provides some information but in my own mind I really don't think that he can support it. Do I go ahead and do the return? Similarly, at what point in time do you call this investment company a liar? Are we 100 percent sure that it wasn't a mistake? To me the possibility is always present. It's difficult to say, "I know you're lying to me" when I'm not 100 percent sure.

From the telephone conversation, Randy explained they did distribute the money out of the IRA so that the client could take advantage of some averaging provisions. In other words, a once-in-a-lifetime deal is going to save this guy a tremendous amount of money. It's a great situation. From what you can tell, in fact, he's probably recommended it to other clients. Now that's the story Kevin heard in phone conversation number one. And I suppose that could be an error. Maybe Randy really never got the advice from the tax counsel that he thought he did, and so maybe he never did transfer the documentation. However, that is difficult to believe after he has described in some detail everything that has happened. Not only does Randy confirm the situation, but in fact, he is very proud of it because it's a great planning idea.

Comment:

An interesting observation that was mentioned previously regarding ethics courses is that rather than learning to become more ethical, we learn to justify with more exotic means that which we wanted to do anyway, which was probably unethical. Specifically in the tax practice, we become very adept at being able to justify our actions by precise readings of the statute. For example, perhaps a position could be taken that, in fact, a distribution was not made because Randy was acting without the authority of his principal. Any actions taken by the broker without instruction from the principal is, in fact, an error. Maybe the investment company did some manipulating with Joe's money for which they had no authority. Maybe Randy never gave him instructions as to what to do. Could it be a mistake of some kind? Possibly, but the fact of the matter is that the CPA cannot prepare the return by just ignoring the problem. That is a blatant error.

Now, much of the problem lies in the "after the fact" situations. If you were aware of the issue during the planning stages, advice could be offered to alleviate many problems. But what about a situation where the incident has already taken place and it appears that someone is really going to be hurt. One little paper transaction can suddenly eliminate possibly half of what this guy is worth. The CPA could ignore the issue, justifying that his client could sue and recover his money from the investment company. This is very tempting, but is it an acceptable attitude? People do things which are totally crazy. Even small changes can result in a tax consequence which is drastic.

Comment:

First of all, I don't know exactly what went on at the broker company, or what transaction actually took place. To me, as a CPA, I would be inclined to believe that they had actually done what they claimed to have done. As far as I know a distribution was made. For him to come back later and say that the 1099-R has been issued in error is unacceptable, regardless of the client's health and mental stability. I'm either preparing a return with the $280,000 in tax or I'm not preparing the return, because I think there's too much exposure involved and it's not my mistake. There's nothing that I did wrong.

Stewart:

What if it had been your mistake? What if you told him to do it? Then would you have made a different decision?

Comment:

Often, a client gets a little bit greedy in maybe making a decision based on the immediacy of the moment, only to find out later that the circumstances are not as they had once appeared. Could there be any additional facts as to Joe's motivation? Perhaps he wanted to get a better rate of return on his money. Such knowledge would confirm that this was not a mistake or that this is truly the first time you know about it. Any discussions with you at any point indicating that the client knew what was going on and it was done with his consent would potentially negate the idea of a true error. It seems like there may be some additional facts embedded in this case.

I think it's not the CPA's mistake, assuming he's never met or heard or known about Randy until he talked to him on the phone for the first time. In addition, the client confirms that he was contacted and he was aware of the decisions and actions of the investment company.

Comment:

Quite often clients will enter into a transaction thinking that they'll get some benefits, particularly higher rates of returns, but when you sit down and explain to them what the consequences are they'll say, "Well, we never really meant to do that to begin with."

In most cases the client is just taking the advice of his investment broker whom he trusts implicitly.

Comment:

I am not convinced that I have an obligation that goes beyond the facts that have been presented to me. If I get a corrected or amended 1099-R, it seems to me that I don't necessarily ever have to get to the question of improper behavior. I don't think we're expected to go back and look into the issues of all 1099-Rs. I'll bet that fifty percent of the K-1s we get are wrong. Such returns are constantly getting corrected and amended. I don't feel an obligation to go beyond this. Now there is a possibility that a distribution was made incorrectly, but I'm not so sure at this point that I have an obligation to go any further. And if I get a corrected 1099-R, why am I not justified in accepting that?

Stewart:

Now, assume that I know that the stated facts are not true. Is that my problem? Do we only have to live up to the law and not what's right? We don't need more laws to tell us all what we should and shouldn't do. We ought to do certain things simply because they're right.

Comment:

We know that the broker said, "We made the distribution because we knew it was in our client's best interest to do it, and our counsel gave us their recommendation. Now, the investment firm adds: P.S. if you want to have an investigation done of all our records, you will find that when somebody examines our records and finds that the distribution was made and then it was undone and corrected, it will be difficult to track down, because most people can't understand a broker's records anyway. But once somebody does understand it, they'll find that a distribution had been made. Now with these facts, we've got a serious problem. Kevin's concern is that when he talked to Randy, he's the one who nearly suggested, 'there better be an error found or you're the ones who are going to come up with the money.'

Comment:

I think a lot of people could make the argument that it's their problem. If they're playing games, they're the ones who are playing the games and I don't care. I've got the 1099 here that says that it's okay. So I file it in with the information that I have, and I'm okay. If anybody did something wrong, I'm clean.

Comment:

In reading this case, I came to the conclusion that we clearly could not file the return by excluding the amount of income. That's an untenable position and we couldn't be a party to it. I can accept the proposition that Joe was totally oblivious to all these crazy rules. All he knew was that his broker said, "Hey, this is a great idea. I think you ought to take a distribution." And Joe said, "If that's what you think I ought to do, Randy, then by all means, let's do it."

Now, Joe could do several things. One possibility is: He could request a ruling and extend his return and perhaps even file his return late.

Another possibility might be to file his return and completely disclose all the facts — everything that Randy said, what Randy did — disclose it and not report it.

A third possibility might be to file the return "the correct way." File it with the initial $280,000 and file a claim for refund showing all the facts. That would be a discussion with the client, with his counsel and with Randy's counsel. However, filing the return based on the amended 1099-R is out of the question.

Comment:

Specifically, Joe can file a request for ruling from the IRS claiming that he didn't know there was going to be a problem. Joe must explain, "I didn't have understanding of the facts, it wasn't explained to me by my broker. All my broker did was transfer it out of one account into another account, and I request that you rule that it's not taxable income." Most likely, the IRS will deny such a request. Joe's only possibility might be to say, "I understand what the law is, the law is clear, but due to the facts and my situation, I would be willing to rely on the mercy of the jury. I'm going to litigate this issue, but I will give you, the IRS, a chance to rule on it in advance." That's one possibility.

The second possibility is to actually litigate as opposed to just requesting an IRS ruling. But in order to have the basis for litigation, Joe must take the position on his return. He then must include all the disclosures in the return, and all the statements in the return, to avoid any penalties. If the return never gets examined, then there is no problem. But if it does, he'll be prepared to litigate it and he will also be willing to get Randy's counsel to pay for the costs of litigation.

The third approach, which may be the best approach, is to file the return, pay the additional tax and file a claim for refund. Then when the IRS disallows that claim for refund, litigate it. Take it to district court and rely on the mercy of the jury.

Stewart:

But suppose he doesn't do any of those three options. He just simply files the return.

Comment:

I think the only person upon whom there could be any fraud would be Randy because he did it with intent. Joe did not act with intent. So there is no fraud on Joe's part.

Comment:

However, if all the facts are explained to Joe and he signs that return, I suspect he is guilty of fraud. Granted he didn't enter into the transaction with the intent of evading tax, but after all the facts are explained to him, he did sign the return. I think he's guilty of fraud along with the accountant who signed it.

Stewart:

What would you report in the return?

Comment:

I'd include in the tax return a copy of both 1099-Rs — the corrected and the wrong one. I'd report no income, but I'd show the 1099s and indicate what I assumed to be the corrected copy. Then, I'd sign the return and attach it.

Stewart:

But you know that is wrong. Could you somehow include prior conversation with the broker?

Comment:

That's why I suggest going for a ruling request or litigation in order to get what is fair. Let the courts decide based upon what's right for me and what's right for the government. I'm willing to let the court decide that.

Comment:

You're suggesting a written dialogue of everything that transpired, you're suggesting to include the two 1099s with the return, which is a type of disclosure, whether it meets the full disclosure requirements or not. How far could you push that? In other words, what's the minimum amount of information that you would give the IRS and still feel comfortable?

Comment:

Well, at the very least I would attach the form number for the section 6661 disclosure. This form essentially says, "Attention Mr. Revenue Agent, I've done something that you're not going to agree with and here are all the facts." Just attaching the two 1099-Rs isn't sufficient.

Comment:

Could Joe file the return based on the distribution and file a claim for refund, explaining everything? That way if the IRS doesn't agree with his position, Joe is safe from any penalties.

Comment:

Joe must be aware that filing a claim for refund fraudulently, is just as bad as filing a return fraudulently. However, he will be filing this claim for refund, disclosing all the facts and stating, "I'm willing to litigate this issue. I think this is important enough. The law is unfair in my situation. It's unequitable; it should be the result. Therefore I'm willing to go to court and have a jury find in my favor."

Stewart:

Before we get into the civil procedure course, consider some of the difficulties that this client might struggle with as you tell him all the things that 'we' should do. But, when it comes right down to it, the money for taxes, accounting fees, attorney fees, etc., are coming out of his pocket. You start seeing all of your time and all of the attorney's time and then you look at this person who doesn't have a whole lot of money to begin with. It seems so much easier to do the two 1099s and file zero income. Nobody's hurt and this poor innocent guy isn't any worse off. And that's where you feel or I think most people feel like they really should compromise. Not just this issue. This type of situation happens all the time, when you see people who get caught in a purely paper transaction. They essentially did something with no substance to it. The change was only in form, but because of the way a law is written, the consequences are costly.

Comment:

I'd like to question the fairness of having to pay tax. Often, we are guilty of creating the image that all tax paying is unfair. But, maybe we as other members of society ought to remember that we've got holes in our roads that are not getting fixed because we need that $280,000 to help us fix our roads. The reality is that there's a chunk of money here that is untaxed income, and fairness demands that there be some tax paid on it. The only question is when?

Comment:

Two hundred and eighty thousand is indeed a huge amount and it represents a substantial portion of this individual's wealth. Therefore, having the jury make the decision on the perceived facts of this case is an appropriate alternative. At the same time, there is an element of fairness that requires the money to be income which ought to be taxed.

Many times we make bad decisions. For example, I may buy an automobile that turns out to be a real lemon. Well, I made a bad choice. Here, too, is someone who is making a bad choice. Financially it was not a smart decision, but he has to live with the consequences. He also should assume a sense of responsibility for those kinds of decisions. You can be given advice — good or bad — by a counselor, a financial advisor, but you must live with the consequences. And you need to recognize that you're the one responsible, it's your money, and you've got to be accountable for that decision.

This man is faced with losing half of his wealth for a mistake that his advisor made. Now, ultimately, there's nothing illegal and immoral with just leaving the money in the IRA and letting it come up normally to pay taxes on it. Yet, the original transaction was a mistake and it fell under a classification which made it heavily taxable. To summarize, we've got a situation where laws will not always come up with the just result. Laws are not perfect. They don't fit every situation perfectly and give perfect justice. And that's not unusual. Very often, you have to obey a law for the sake of a law, not because of the great justice in which it results. In this country we've agreed that a system of law and order is the best way to live. And that's the issue to deal with here. How much are willing to pay for upholding the law?

Stewart:

In sum, you're saying that the individual should be taking responsibility for his own acts. But at what point does Joe become the innocent victim of bad advice? Where does his taking responsibility stop and Randy's begin as you see it?

Comment:

I've seen so many people who have been given financial advice concerning investments, which later turn out to be bad. Joe listened to the advice of Randy and Randy gave him bad advice. Now if Randy had been saying, "You ought to invest it in oil wells somewhere" and the oil wells are dry, Joe would have lost the money in the same way. It seems that anyone who is going to be listening to and accepting advice accepts the responsibility for their actions.

Here the issue of fairness is one having to do with tax. However, this is irrelevant because we're dealing with an issue of societal fairness. Is it wrong for this individual to have to pay a tax because the IRS or society has created a ruling that requires it?

Comment:

The point is, that is not some off-the-wall rule. We as society, by way of our elected representatives, decided that $280,000 in tax should be paid in this situation. Congress passed this law, not the IRS.

Stewart:

We seem to have clearly determined that two people in the story have ethical problems. But we haven't talked about another alternative. What kind of an ethical problem does Joe have? Suppose he says, "I don't want Randy to do anything more about it. I want him to file an amended 1099-R. I don't want Kevin to do anything about it, either. You've all let me down. I've paid for your advice and it was wrong. I did not intend this result and I am immeasurably harmed because of it. In fact, I'll file my own darn return from now on." Now what kind of an ethical issue does Joe have? He might say, "I am going to file and I am not going to report it because it was a mistake of facts. I was misled. Therefore, a mistaken fact precludes me from having responsibility." Is that an ethical issue?

Comment:

Michael Josephson brought up another interesting question. What if the auditor for the investment company picks up on the transaction? What are his responsibilities when he sees it going in and coming out again? What do you do then? And maybe it's not just this one transaction. What if he finds a dozen or more? Randy could have advised all their clients to do exactly the same thing.

Comment:

Assume for a moment that we know the transaction was made, that we don't buy that there was an error, and that we know that Joe owes the $280,000. And now Joe says, "Hey, I don't like the way you're going to do my return. I'm going to do it myself." Although, now that he's preparing the return, it's not a CPA signing it. We're not culpable, nor are we negligent because we're not the preparer of the return. As a CPA, do we have any obligation to do anything more if we know that he's committing a tax fraud?

Comment:

This is an ethical question, not a pragmatic one, what do you do in a practice situation? I'm raising the issue: what do we do when we know that a client has committed a wrongful act, be it tax fraud, or some other kind of fraud that we haven't prepared or signed but we know of his involvement. Ethically, what do we do?

Comment:

The real question comes at what point do we quit being the client's conscience? Some say that the point at which we don't do the return is where we no longer have a conscience in regards to that situation. However, I'm not sure that's were we can draw the line. I'm very reluctant to go to my client and say, "Client, you're lying to me," because I don't know 100 percent. You have to rely on what he tells you. Which 1099 do I know is the mistake? I don't have the facts to determine which story is wrong. Was the first 1099 wrong? Or was the telephone conversation wrong?

Comment:

Remember that I don't have to have proof that the client is lying to me. If I'm confident that he's lying to me, I just won't do his work. It's a relatively easy solution. I don't want to question whether a client is going to tell me the truth or whether he's going to lie to me. If I question that, it's a very easy solution for me. He's not my client anymore.

Comment:

That is an easy solution if you're making $80,000 but it's not so simple for a person who is making $10,000 doing tax returns. If you're making $80,000, then it's easier to tell that $200 client to find another accountant. That's not to say that only the wealthy can afford to be ethical, but I do think it's tougher to make the decision when an added financial pressure exists.

Comment:

In similar situations which I have encountered I have literally typed up a letter to the client, signed it, and given it to him to sign. The letter explains that even though I think the story is a little gray, the client can do what he chooses. And if he says, "No, I did it right." Then I say, "Okay, I've given you a rule, I've done everything I can. You signed it. What more can I do?"

Comment:

You can only talk to him. If the client keeps saying, "No, I'm doing it straight," what can you do? And when you only have a $10,000 practice, you just try to do everything as ethically as you can. They say they're following the rules. And you keep reading the rules. You just have to make sure that they understand the applicable rules.

Stewart:

But how do you know they're clean?

Comment:

With cash you don't know. In some situations unless you're doing a detailed audit, you don't know what has actually happened. Unless you're auditing everything or watching the cash drawer, there are some things people can hide from you . You can't see it all.

Comment:

I think we all know that we're not responsible to go that far. But some claims are just not reasonable. Travel and entertainment is an obvious one. Often, the expense is incredible compared to the amount of income that the client actually generated. It's possible, I suppose, but it's unlikely that they would incur those kinds of expenses.

Comment:

I tell them I think it's unreasonable. I tell them that the IRS has come out with guidelines on such expenses. If it's too vagrant, I won't do it. But I literally don't review the whole file.

Stewart:

The issues that have been raised thus far cover many different ethical areas. Originally, we discussed what to do when you know there's a problem. Now, there is a different issue to consider. We're not auditors for the IRS. We prepare our tax return information based on information that is given to us by the client. We sign that return signifying that to the best of our knowledge, based on the information given by the client, this return is right. The client then signs the return and says that the information he provided was basically right. Similar to an automobile deduction, you must have written evidence to support the claim. The client should confirm that he has the evidence in written form should the need for proof arise. Is there anything other than advice that should be given to Kevin?

Basically, I'd call Joe into my office and say, "Joe, you have a problem with your investment company. Now you'd better get with them and get it resolved." I don't think as the CPA, I should be in the middle of the situation, unless Joe wants to pay for my services. If he says, "I don't understand what they're telling me, so please work it out." I'll say, "Fine. I'll do it for $75 an hour. I'll talk to them and resolve the issue to the best of my ability."

Questions

1. If you have some communication with the client in this case, how extensive should it be?
2. To what extent should Kevin get involved with the financial planner? Should he have called Randy in the first place?
3. When and where should a compromise be involved with tax rulings? Should a compromise be considered in this case?

9
Ethical Issues in the Practice of Management Consulting

DR. J. OWEN CHERRINGTON
Dr. Cherrington earned his M.B.A. and doctorate degrees at the University of Minnesota with major emphasis in accounting and management information systems. He is currently a professor of accounting at Brigham Young University. During 1989 he worked with Arthur Young as a management consultant and has developed seminars and cases on ethics.

Introduction

To some people, "ethics" in "consulting" is a contradiction of terms. It is an oxymoron like a "fun run," "simplified tax code," or "funny accountant." Other people view consultants as carrying a very large bag of tricks, almost like a Santa Claus bag. Whatever a client wants or is in the mood to buy, the consultant is ready to sell. Nevertheless, this chapter is titled: "Ethical Issues in the Practice of Management Consulting."

The ethical issues that face consulting as a profession within public accounting are quite different from the ethical issues that individual consultants face in their everyday work environment. I want to touch on both sets of issues.

The scope of services and its impact on firm organization, our code of ethics, and independence ought to be the most important ethical issues that we face as a profession. Every accountant ought to be concerned with the recent internal problems of some of what we used to call the "Big Eight" accounting firms. The desire of the consulting divisions to split-off or to be bought-out, or to require more pay, greater equity, and increased governance are not only issues inherent in the scope of practice, but are the basic issues of power, equity, and fairness.

Most consultants, however, do not identify the scope of services as their most pressing ethical issue. When asked, "What ethical issues

---

Reprinted by permission of Dr. J. Owen Cherrington.

do you face in your work as a consultant?" most responses are in the areas of honesty, fairness in working with fellow employees, providing a quality service to clients, charging a fair price, and placing the client's interest above their own.

History and Current Climate in Public Accounting _____

I want to first discuss the scope of services issue. Let me begin by reviewing some of the history of public accounting and try to describe the current climate of management consulting in public accounting.

History of Public Accounting

Most large public accounting firms started in the late 1800's. Initially, a very large part of their services would be classified as management consulting in today's terminology. Arthur Young, the founder of the firm by the same name, was trained as an attorney and came in contact with the world of accounting during his apprenticeship. In 1884 he writes:

> That law office had a great number of trust estates, and looking after those estates was a large part of their business.... We had to see not only that the books of each trust were in order, but we had to examine the published reports of many companies in which the various trusts had investments. The result was that the law firm consulted not only stockbrokers but also chartered accountants before deciding about the selling or buying of investments....[1]

This would probably be classified as financial planning in today's terminology.

Let me read a couple of advertisements from *The Book-Keeper*, a weekly magazine published in New York, on November 23, 1880.

> *Selden R. Hopkins*
> *Consulting and Expert Accounting,*
> *Office 94 Liberty St., N.Y.*
>
> *Will render assistance to lawyers in the examination of accounts in litigation; aid agents and administrators of estates in adjusting accounts.*

Today we would classify this as litigation support.

> *Will give council upon improved methods of keeping the accounts of corporated companies. Assist book-keepers and business men in*

---

[1] *Arthur Young & Co.* "Arthur Young: The Man Behind the Name," Summer, 1980, p. 16.

straightening out intricate and improperly kept books. Adjust compli-cated partnership accounts. Examine books for stockholders and creditors.

That paragraph has a little systems analysis and design, accounting, and auditing.

All work entrusted to me will be promptly attended to, and considered in strict confidence.[2]

WM. H. VEYSEY
Professional Accountant,
No. 150 Broadway, Rm. 90
Corner of Liberty St., New York

Books opened and arranged for all classes of business in the most simple and concise manner.

This is more systems analysis and design.

The rigid investigation of complicated and disputed matters, and the clear presentation of the results, divested of technicality, a specialty.

Particular attention given to the books of insurance companies, and to accounts of executors, estates in trust and bankrupt estates.[3]

This is more litigation support.

An analysis of these and other advertisements indicates a variety of services including; bookkeeping, investigations, litigation support, teaching, and audits of businesses usually as a result of business failure.

Although it is difficult to determine average revenues generated from each service provided by public accountants during this early period, the results of one British accounting firm, Whinney Smith and Whinney, is available for 1880 and again for 1905.[4] Fees were generated from the following sources in 1880:

72% from insolvency,
11% from accounting,
10% from auditing, and
  6% from trusteeship, taxation, executorship, and special work.

These numbers changed significantly over the next 25 years. In 1905 their fees were generated from the following sources:

---

[2]Robert Mednick and Gary John Previts, "The Scope of CPA Services: A View of the Future from the Perspective of a Century of Progress," *Journal of Accountancy,* (May, 1987), p. 222.
[3]*Ibid.*
[4]*Ibid.*

> 17% from insolvency,
> 13% from accounting,
> 58% from auditing,
> 1% or less from taxation work,
> 5% in trusteeship, and
> 5% in governmental or special work.

The biggest gain was in auditing which increased from 10% to 58%. This gain came almost entirely from insolvency which decreased from 72% to 17%. This rapid shift in services in the United Kingdom can largely be attributed to a shift in demand as the new industrialized society demanded an independent affirmation of financial information to evaluate the operations of new corporate enterprises.

These early writings and statistics are interesting because they indicate that public accounting practices were largely what we classify today as consulting firms. Their specialty was financial information. Anything that dealt with the development, interpretation, and use of financial information seemed to be an acceptable engagement for these firms.

Change in the Scope of Practice _____

Legislation in the United States had a significant impact on the scope of services offered by U. S. accounting firms during the middle portion of this century. The federal corporate excise tax law of 1909 and the individual income tax law of 1913 created a need for tax-type consulting. Early CPA leaders assisted the Treasury Department and other government officials in defining policy for measuring taxable income so that initial regulations were consistent with the books and records of the business community. Tax compliance and tax planning developed out of these and subsequent laws. The tax practice in CPA firms has grown as the tax laws have become more, and more complicated.

Probably the most significant legislation for accountants was the Securities Act of 1933 and the Securities and Exchange Act of 1934. These laws require companies whose stock is sold publicly to be listed with the Securities and Exchange Commission and have their financial statements audited by independent Certified Public Accountants. This requirement, along with the growth in our industrial economy, created a very large need for auditing services. As a result, public accounting firms became known almost entirely as "auditing firms" throughout most of the 1940's, 1950's, and 1960's. Work was so plentiful that public accounting firms stopped most marketing and selling activities. In fact, it was considered unprofessional to advertise and openly market services.

Much of what we know today as accounting was developed during this period of time; when auditing was the predominate service in public accounting. Therefore, things like the AICPA Code of Ethics has been very much biased toward auditing. This must have been evident to the 1983 Special Committee on Standards of Professional Conduct for Certified Public Accountants because they concluded, "It is clear that the Code requires broadening and changing to meet developments in the profession's environment."[5]

The product life cycle for audited financial statements has been relatively long compared to most products. However, the growth and profitability of the audit compared to other services offered by CPA firms has slipped significantly in recent years. Most firms obtain only about 55% to 60% of their revenues from audit, down from 70% to 80% only a few years ago. For Arthur Andersen, only 47% of their revenues are currently generated from auditing. Consulting and tax services have both increased to the point that they currently provide about 20% of firm revenues.[6]

Factors of Change in the Accounting Profession

Risk, growth, and profitability are other important factors causing a change in product mix. First, *risk*: Potential losses in litigation settlements associated with failed companies which previously received a clean audit opinion are tremendous. This discourages accepting new audit work for questionable organizations. Quoting from a Forbes article:

> Arthur Andersen alone has been tagged with a reported $137 million in pay-outs in recent years and now admits to refusing more and more "audit risks" out of fear of more litigation. [7]

Second, *growth*: The merger boom in recent years has had a depressive effect on audit growth and the increased need for analysis and design of information systems has boosted consulting revenues. Quoting again from the Forbes article:

> The problem ... is that each of the mergers results in a net loss of audit dollars.... The audit fee of two combined firms in a merger is about 65% of the combined audit fees of the two firms taken independently, ... Thus, the firms have been chasing after smaller and smaller corporate clients. [8]

---

[5]Special Committee on Standards of Professional Conduct for Certified Public Accountants, *Restructuring Professional Standards to Achieve Professional Excellence in a Changing Environment.* (New York, N.Y.: AICPA, 1986), p. 21.

[6]Richard Greene, "Blood on the Ledger," *Forbes*, May 18, 1987, p. 204.

[7]Ibid. pp. 203-204.

[8]Ibid. p. 204.

Quoting from a *Wall Street Journal* article in July of 1988:

> *Consulting revenues are ballooning at an average 30% annual rate, about double the growth of auditing and tax work....*
>
> *Information-systems consulting revenues are exploding, with 40% annual growth, compared with only 17% to 18% for total firm revenues.*[9]

Third, *profitability*: Profitability data is difficult to obtain and the results seem to vary significantly from firm to firm. In general, profits of most firms are down primarily due to heavy discounting of audit fees and low-balling to obtain new audit clients. Consulting in certain practice areas of some firms has become very profitable as reflected in the following quotation published by the *Wall Street Journal.*

> *...one of the problems for consulting partners at Andersen is that "we contribute almost twice as much as auditing and tax partners to gross profits after deducting salaries and other costs. ...after litigation costs, Andersen's audit practice loses money, and the tax practice is only "marginally profitable.*[10]

These circumstances have created discord primarily between auditors and consultants. The auditors point back in time only five to ten years when audit and tax tended to carry consulting, which at that time wasn't covering start-up costs. Consultants point to current growth, risk, and profitability and demand higher compensation, greater equity, and more governance in running the business.

Let me summarize the history and current status of public accounting with several key points:

1. Public accounting firms as they began to develop 70 to 100 years ago were primarily financial consulting firms.

2. Government legislation created the need for tax and auditing, which became the dominant services provided during much of the current century.

3. Recent years have seen a decline in the dominance and profitability of auditing and a corresponding increase in the dominance and profitability of consulting.

4. We are currently in this shifting state with consultants demanding higher compensation, greater equity, and more governance in the operation of the firm.

---

[9]"Cutting the Pie: Accounting Firms Face a Deepening Division Over Consultant's Pay," *Wall Street Journal,* July 26, 1988, p. 1.

[10]Ibid.

Ethics of the Profession — According to the Literature _____

Most of the ethical issues in published literature center around the scope of services and the code of ethics that was developed primarily for an audit practice. The scope of services issue according to the literature is this:

Can a CPA firm maintain its independence for auditing financial statements while it is doing other consulting work for the same company?

There are several groups of people that have an interest in this issue including competitors, regulators, CPA firms, and clients. Competitors and some regulators have been the most vocal on this issue. One competitor writes:

Is your accounting firm still an accounting firm? At what point are accounting firms really accounting firms in name only?[11]

Another competitor points out that:

...because the manipulation of corporate numbers is handled by information systems, the certifiers of the rectitude of those manipulations should not be the people who designed the systems and the software that runs them.[12]

A comment by Representative John Dingell, chairman of the House Subcommittee on Oversight and Investigations clearly reflects the concerns of regulators:

Independence is the one essential trait claimed by auditors that separates them from other professions. However, it is natural to ask how independent anybody can be when that person is hired, fired and paid by the people being audited. When I hear of low-ball audit fees, of audits used as loss leaders to attract consulting business, that non-audit work is the wave of the future or that the top partners at major audit firms are management consultants, I frankly do not understand how that enhances the accounting profession's unique reputation for independent judgment as a public service.[13]

Accounting firms argue that the central issue is whether public accounting should be allowed to evolve in response to users' needs. They suggest that the expansion has been natural and in areas akin to traditional practice and that a dynamic profession cannot continue to thrive in a changing world if its scope of activities is confined by

[11]Mark Stevens, "Is Your Accounting Firm Still an Accounting Firm?" *Financial Executives*, July, 1985, p. 24.

[12]Parker Hodges, "Do the Big Eight Add Up?" *Datamation*, February 15, 1987, p. 64.

[13]Mark Stevens, "No More White Shoes" *Business Month*, April, 1988, p. 41.

rigid, arbitrary rules. With the benefit of hindsight and experience, they argue that the alleged problems related to scope of practice did not, and do not exist, and that there is nothing broken that requires fixing. No one has pointed to any specific situation in present practice where performance on a consulting engagement has jeopardized audit independence.[14]

The attitude of users of accounting services has been obtained by a recent survey conducted by the Public Oversight Board. Of the respondents, 12% said: "CPAs should be allowed to perform a full range of management advisory services because impairment of audit independence and objectivity is not a problem." About 75% agreed that "CPAs should be allowed to perform only those management services where it is clear that audit independence and objectivity cannot be impaired." Only 9% believe CPAs should not be allowed to perform management advisory services.

The users seemed to be very perceptive in identifying services that tend to impair audit independence. For example, 76% felt that negotiating mergers, acquisitions, and divestitures caused a "great deal of" or "some" impairment of independence. On the reverse side, 73% felt that designing a computer system posed "little" to "no" chance of impairing audit independence.[15]

The appropriate scope of services is not a new issue. In 1925, A. P. Richardson, the *Journal's* editor, discussed two schools of thought developing in the profession:

> *(One) ... school is more aggressive and ready to spread into fields new and untried and in short to do all things which may seem to be required by a client whether those things are of accountancy or otherwise. The (other) school has taken as its motto ... "Let the cobbler stick to his last."*[16]

Arthur Andersen, the founder of the firm carrying his name, was outspoken on this issue. In an address given by him at the Institute's 1925 regional meeting he said:

> *In the experience of the past 10 years, the businessman has found that advice from an accounting viewpoint may have high cash value in the form of taxes saved or refunded, war contracts liquidated, (etc.)... The present-day accountant who is alert will grasp after every opportunity to foster this attitude by increasing the constructive value of all normal work in seeking newer and better fields of service to business management.... In filling the function of advisor or consultant to*

---

[14]William D. Hall, "An Acceptable Scope of Practice," *The CPA Journal*, February, 1988, pp. 24-33.

[15]Louise Dratler Haberman, "Beyond the Audit: MAS," *New Accountant*, January, 1987, pp. 20-21.

[13]Mednick and Previts, op. cit., p. 224.

> *management the accountant is thus entering fields of investigative*
> *work which mark a distinctive advance over the earlier conceptions of*
> *the scope of his service and which deal with the broad aspects of*
> *business as a whole.... It is my profound conviction that the accoun-*
> *tant of the future will prosper and consolidate his position in the*
> *business world in proportion to his breadth of vision and willingness*
> *to accept his responsibility of larger service to industry.*[17]

Impact on Independence

The impact of this broadened scope of services on audit independence was heavily discussed during the 1950's and has been an issue ever since. The fact that the problem does not go away suggests to me that it is a real problem; that certain consulting services should not be performed for audit clients. Services resulting in self-audits and involving management decision-making create a loss of independence, if not in fact, at least in perception, and should be avoided. Great care should be exercised in venturing into new services, especially those removed from our traditional areas of expertise. There must be a central core and common mission that holds the parts of our practice together and makes the whole function effectively.

The independence issue relating to scope of service for me is minor compared to the conflict that it is causing within our public accounting firms. The desire, and almost greed, expressed by some consultants for more money, greater equity, and increased governance have the potential of breaking apart public accounting as we know it today. In my view, consultants need to curb their desire for quick fixes to very difficult issues. On the other hand, equity and fairness requires rewards in the form of pay, equity, and governance to be given according to performance. Therefore, auditors and tax personnel must be willing to adjust and recognize the changes that have occurred and are occurring.

My view of public accounting is rather broad, and more in the mold of public accounting firms 70 to 100 years ago. If you accept this view, then there are many ethical issues yet to be resolved. For example:

1. How do we define CPA and present it to the public so that we do not mislead them? Many of those working for CPA firms, and some who are leaders in the firms, are not CPAs. I don't think the common business person understands this. For me, that is misleading and something that the profession must address.

2. How do we organize our accounting firms and determine pay and ownership equity so it is fair to all employees?

---

[17]*Ibid.* p. 224-225.

3. How do we structure our practice and our code of ethics so that they are consistent with respect to non-CPAs as partners. Our current code of ethics allows firms who put "CPA" on their letterhead to only count CPAs as partners. To get around this, non-CPAs are called principals, yet they share in salary, bonuses, and other leadership roles within the firm the same as CPA partners.[18] When these non-CPA principals are introduced to potential clients, they are usually called partners.

A bill currently before the Missouri House of Representatives would allow CPAs to enter into partnerships with non-CPAs. Under the bill, a CPA and an unlicensed accountant would be able to operate a partnership and advertise it as a CPA firm. The partnership would not have to designate which partner was a CPA nor would the participating CPA have to be licensed to practice in Missouri. Needless to say, the Missouri Society of CPAs is vigorously lobbying against the bill.[19]

The other ethical issues frequently discussed in the literature include advertising, contingent fees, and commissions. Much that has been written on these topics is not relevant today due to recent modifications in the AICPA Code of Ethics. Clearly, the avoidance of contingent fees and commissions are important elements in maintaining audit independence, but they are not as relevant for consulting. Advertising must always be done in good taste to maintain a professional image.

New Ethical Issues

However, the changes that have occurred in these areas, create a new set of ethical issues. For example:

- How do we advertise so as not to mislead, to accurately reflect our capabilities, and to present a professional image?

- How should contingent fees be structured so they are fair for the client and provide a fair return for our services?

- How can we accept commissions without completely destroying our independence and objectivity? If we accept a commission without the client knowing about it, we are unethical because we have misled them. They assumed we were unbiased and objective, when we were not. Once we tell them we receive a commission and are not unbiased or independent, we become as other salesmen; at least for that particular service.

---

[17]Stevens, op. cit. p. 40.

[18]"Missouri Society Lobbies Against Bill to Allow CPAs to Enter Partnerships with Non-CPAs," *Public Accounting Report*, Vol. XII No. 9, May 1, 1989, p. 1.

Let me give an example of this. I received in the mail an invitation to "join with" a financial group that sells stocks, bonds, and other financial services. This was their proposal:

> *we envision in our working relationship: (1) You become licensed and registered for investment and insurance sales — a process we'll help you with; (2) You agree fully to comply with the latest AICPA standards governing receipt of contingency fees and commissions; (3) You work through us either on a referral basis or your own direct sales, in providing financial products and service to your clients; and (4) You receive, upon the sale of any such product, a percentage of the gross commission.*[20]

If I were to join this group, I would hope my clients would not view me as unbiased in the financial investments I recommend. But, having lost my objectivity in recommending financial investments, I will *probably in my client's mind lose* my objectivity in other services I render. I don't think the client will be able to differentiate when we are independent and when we are not, and we will completely lose our reputation of independence.

Ethical Issues as Viewed by Individual Consultants

Let me move to the last section of this topic dealing with the ethical issues that individual consultants face in performing their work. In preparation, I interviewed approximately 50 management consultants in CPA firms. Those interviewed came from all levels; staff, senior, manager, partner, even one partner in charge of the regional consulting practice of the firm. In general, the ethical issues in management consulting addressed in the literature are quite different than those identified by the practicing consultant. Only four individuals identified scope of practice, independence, and advertising as important ethical issues in the performance of their work.

I have classified their comments into four areas; personal integrity, marketing, expense reporting, and providing a quality product.

Honesty. Several of the issues described to me were nothing more than decisions to tell the truth or to lie. One consultant made the following comment:

> *Frequently on a consulting engagement I am asked a question so I need to return a comment. When should I tell the truth and when should I lie is a problem for me. Recently a client retained us to develop a new information system which will replace several employees. The client asked us not to mention anything to employees about the impact of the*

---

[20]G. L. Leavitt Financial Group, A Letter Addressed to Mr. Cherrington, Received May, 1989.

new system on employee jobs. When employees ask me about potential job displacement, do I lie as requested, or tell the truth and go against the client's wishes?

Another employee said:

We have regular progress reports with the client. The project group leader continues to tell the client we are on schedule and will complete the project by the specified date when everyone on the team knows it will not be achieved. When the client asks me how things are going, what should I say?

A third employee had a slightly different problem:

I'm bidding on a multi-million dollar project that will extend over a three-year time period. I really think the project will cost $4.75 million, but I don't think the client will commit to the project at anything more than $4.0 million. Since it is a time and expense fee structure, I can bid $4.0 million to get started. After we are a year or two into the project I can inform them of the expected over-run. By then they will be so far into the project they won't terminate it for the $.75 million extra. I really think this is a great project for us as well as for the client. Am I acting ethically?

Marketing and Selling Work. There is tremendous pressure in the consulting environment to sell new work. The ethical issue is: Where should the consultant's first allegiance lie — to the firm or to the client? Should the first allegiance be to the consulting firm to sell new work, or to the client and what is perceived to be in their best interest? This conflict is described in the following situations:

I am developing an information system for a client. The client knows me and trusts me. An additional module for the system would be "nice to have" and profitable for us. But the client doesn't really "need" it. I know the client would buy it if I proposed it. Should I propose it?

Another consultant described a similar problem:

The system we are developing has many modules to handle various contingencies. We can leave out a few modules, or make it difficult to handle some contingencies. This gives us an opportunity to sell add-on work, which is good for us, but I'm not sure it is fair for the client.

One consultant questioned the ethics of assisting in developing a Request for Proposal (RFP) and later bidding on that proposal:

Many people consider it "good business" to help a client develop an RFP for consulting work. You have an inside-track, so to speak, on the client's needs which helps you in writing a better proposal. But more important, you can slant the RFP toward the services that you can offer best. Is it really ethical to assist in developing an RFP, to which you later respond?

Accurate Expense Reporting. The firms from which the interviews were taken have very detailed rules for handling expenses. Yet this issue continues to raise multiple ethics issues:

> *There are a lot of costs associated with your work as a consultant. Frequently, it is difficult to know which I should cover out of my own money, which should be charged to the client, and which should be charged to new business development. For example, I took a group of client employees to lunch to improve our working relationships and to report project status. How should I handle the cost of the lunch?*

Another example:

> *I'm living "out-of-town" for an extended period of time to work on a large systems engagement. Is it fair for me to be reimbursed for my living and travel expenses even though I am single, own no house, and don't really have a "home"?*

A third example:

> *The secretary bought an airplane ticket for my weekend trip home. However, because I had to work late, I personally rebooked my ticket. Since it was a later flight, the airfare was less and I was reimbursed for the difference. What should I do with the money?*

A slightly different problem with expense reporting came from another consultant:

> *I'm on an out-of-town assignment which provides a daily per diem to cover food and laundry. Some members of the consulting team went out for lunch together and the partner-in-charge picked up the tab. I adjusted my per diem, but I know three members of the team who claimed a full day per diem on their time and expense report. What should I do?*

Providing a Quality Service for a Fair Price. Most consultants seem to struggle daily with the quality of service being provided and the fairness of the amount charged to the client:

> *I'm on a systems project with our fee determined by "time and materials." The speed and efficiency of my staff have an important impact on the length of the engagement, and the amount of our fee. I have faced several issues lately that are ethics-related:*
>
> • *Intentionally lengthening out one engagement to better match the termination of this project with the start of the next project.*
>
> • *Incompetence of my staff because many of them are new hires and lack experience with this type of project. Of course the client wants to have the most qualified people working on their projects. But, the consulting firm needs*

to keep its people busy on chargeable work that develops their abilities in a variety of areas. We still get the work done, but it takes longer and costs the client more money. How do I balance the needs of the firm with the needs of the client on these staffing issues?

- *I am occasionally assigned to do a job for which I am not qualified. I have to spend some time in study to prepare myself to do a good job. Is it fair for me to charge my client for that time?*

Another consultant expressed concern over the accuracy of time-keeping:

Time is the basis to bill the client on most of our jobs. During the day my productive time is interrupted by a variety of things — a call from a different client, a supervisor asking about progress on a different project, and fellow workers discussing non-work related items. I feel like I should accurately report my time on each job, no more and no less. How do I do it without spending all my time counting minutes?

A managing partner had concern about both quality and profit:

We commit to something and then we try to figure out how to do it. It seems like there ought to be some parameters that outline what we do and use as a basis to either accept or reject an engagement. This is not only an ethical issue of quality, it is also a profit issue. Sometimes it costs us three times what we receive in fees to do a quality job.

One consultant described a "Can I Get Away With It?" attitude:

Many consultants seem to have the attitude that you should "do what you can do as long as you can get away with it." What is my responsibility to my co-workers, supervisor, or subordinates when I see this attitude expressed? Recently I reported a major problem on a big project to upper management of our firm. The response was, "Don't worry about it, the client is still paying the bill."

One last comment:

I'm working on a systems project with our fee based on time and materials. Am I supposed to design the system to make the consulting partner look good, or a system that is best for the client? Who is my client on this project?

Many of these ethical dilemmas have no easy solutions. However, there are some common principles that I have found are important in determining an appropriate response:

1st Honesty is synonymous with good business practice. Any short-run profits from dishonest acts are minor compared to lost opportunity in the long-run.

2nd Solve the problem early. Any misunderstanding or misrepresentation can be corrected much easier if it is addressed early. As time passes, it becomes much more difficult and costly to correct the problem.

3rd Consider the impact of full information on both sides of the agreement. An important question for me is; "If the other party had all the information I have, how would they feel about it?" If I don't know how they would feel, I feel some obligation to provide that information to them and openly discuss the issue.

4th Consider the counsel a spouse or other family member would provide on the situation. Since my activities reflect positively or negatively on them, I find I make better ethical decisions when I consider them and their advice.

5th Consider how you would feel if all the facts were published on the front page of the *Wall Street Journal*. Sometimes we make decisions thinking nobody in the world will ever know about this but us. Those are the situations that seem to eventually be made public for everyone to see.

Conclusion

In summary, the ethical issues that face consulting as a profession are quite different than those faced by individual consultants. Scope of service for me is the most important issue facing the consulting profession. It has the potential to split the profession as we know it today and as it has existed for the past 100 years.

The issues that individual consultants face are basic issues of honesty and fairness.

Questions

1. Has the accounting profession changed much over the last 100 years? In what ways has it changed? Why?
2. Why was it necessary for the government to legislate the Securities Act of 1933 and the Securities and Exchange Act of 1934?
3. Why has audit revenue decreased over the last 10 years? What services will make up for these changes in the future?
4. What are some of the possible independence conflicts resulting between auditors and consultants working for the same client?
5. What possible ethical concerns face today's CPA's? What is your opinion regarding these issues?
6. Are ethics based on a judgment call or are they based on specific ideas and principles? Explain.

10
Ethical Issues in the Practice of System and Management Consulting — A Case

DR. ERIC DENNA

Dr. Denna received his doctoral degree from Michigan State University. He is currently an Assistant Professor in the School of Accountancy at Brigham Young University. He is a member of the AAA and the IIA. His research interests have been in the area of computerized information systems.

Situation

Carla is exhausted as she leans back in her chair. Not only has she put in a tremendous amount of time during the past week, but she has also struggled with a delicate situation involving a valuable client. Carla remembers her days at Ethics University in which a situation like this had been discussed in class. At that time, she was a bit bored by the discussion but now wishes she had listened more attentively. She never imagined she would ever face a similar situation.

Carla was one of the top students in the information systems program at Ethics University and has been heavily recruited by a number of firms. She accepted an offer to join Coopers & Sells (C&S) and during the past eight years has been involved in the analysis and design of retail information systems. She is recognized throughout the firm as an expert in the area of retail information systems.

During the past eight years, Carla has been an EDP specialist to evaluate EDP controls for a number of retail audit engagements for a variety of clients. A number of times she has been allowed access to very sensitive retail installations which were the envy of competitors, including the client with whom she is having the current struggle. Carla signed nondisclosure agreements with each of the clients prior to performing her review function.

Reprinted by permission of Dr. Eric Denna.

Carla's Dilemma _____

A year and a half ago, Carla obtained a contract with We Got It Stores (WGIS) to design and implement a new information system for the entire organization. The fee structure is a cost plus basis and is projected to result in about $15 million in fees to C&S. Carla was a bit nervous about the $15 million bid as she knew there was no way they could keep costs so low. However, the engagement partner insisted that the bid be $15 million; otherwise, they would not get the contract. He said that they would handle the overruns later.

As a result of the WGIS contract alone, she is being considered for partnership two years ahead of her peers, making her the first female to be considered for partnership status and one of the few ever to be considered so early. The final decision is to be made at the partners' meeting next month. A major consideration for her promotion will be the satisfaction of her engagement partner and WGIS management with her work. Fortunately for Carla, the evaluation meeting was not held today.

Earlier this morning she presented WGIS's management with an update on the project. Carla has informed WGIS management that the original cost estimate of $15 million could be exceeded by as much as $5 to even $10 million dollars. She knew she would eventually have to do this when they bid the job. This confirmed what she had suspected at the beginning of the project — that the partner had only wanted to get WGIS deeply into the project before being realistic and letting them know what the costs would actually be.

The second problem Carla faces with WGIS is even more trouble-some than the first. During the presentation, Carla became aware that WGIS awarded the contract to C&S because they knew of Carla's experience in having seen many of the competition's systems. They also made it very clear that they expected her to adopt many of these same features in her work for WGIS. Basically, Carla is being asked to take advantage of experiences and knowledge she has acquired in confidence. To make matters worse, the engagement partner, who also attended the meeting, promised WGIS management that Carla would give them the full benefit of her knowledge and experience.

Although WGIS is a little disturbed about the projected cost overruns, they are insisting that WGIS's information system have the same features they know are in the competition's systems. It is very clear that if these features are not included, WGIS will terminate the contract with C&S and award the contract to Price & Arthur.

1. What should Carla have done regarding the original cost estimate of the WGIS bid? What should she do now?

2. What should Carla do regarding WGIS's insistence that she borrow features from competitors' systems with which she has become acquainted?

3. How should Carla respond to the partner's promise?

4. Is there a framework which can be developed to help Carla and others in similar situations?

5. What are other ethical issues in the practice of management consulting?

Denna:

What should Carla have done regarding the original cost estimate of the client bid? What are some alternatives that Carla could have used at the onset?

Comment:

Carla needed to insist on being realistic in creating a breakdown of expenses. She could have said, "If you want to use my expertise in this project, I insist that we give a realistic estimate of what the costs are going to be and not just go in with the idea of bidding $15 million now and $30 or $40 million later on. If you don't want to do it that way, then go ahead and get somebody else."

Comment:

Going along with the $15 million bid is another alternative — which she apparently has done.

Denna:

It seems that Carla has recognized that she can concede to the plan and just hope that: (1) the partner knows more than her and is really trying to be up front and it works, or (2) hope that someone else has to break the news to the client. What's the criteria for choice? Consider the first alternative: Insist on a realistic bid. In other words, the partner says, "We're going to go with $15 million," and Carla says, "If you want me to work on this, we're going to bid at $20 or $25 million." What could possibly happen there?

Comment:

She could lose her job, depending on the character of the partner, or they could find an alternative way to make the statement work. Professional people are capable of reducing the costs with different labor mixes, better procedures, etc.

Comment:

I don't really know why anybody with her qualifications needs to have that much fear either way. Anybody that's an expert in their field shouldn't fear. If she doesn't stay where she's at, she's certainly got plenty of opportunities elsewhere. The fear must stem from being caught up in the idea of making partner ahead of others her same age. Carla just doesn't realize the strength she's got in terms of her own expertise. She's what the company is marketing to the other client. Coopers & Sells is promising that it's her talents they are going to use. She's in a very powerful position.

Denna:

Put yourself in the partner's position. Carla approaches you and says, "I'm sorry, but I don't feel good about this. I prefer not to be in this engagement unless the bid is increased." How many of us would all of a sudden be able to bid without someone like Carla who obviously has the expertise that we will be dependent upon? How many of us would be willing to bid the job?

Comment:

One dimension of this problem, too, is that we aren't talking about a firm, fixed-price type contract. We're talking about a cost-plus effort in which the client will probably be doing some sort of a cost estimate on the other side. As a result, there could be some influences that may very well come back during the negotiation process that will say, "Are you trying to low ball this thing? We're not going to do business with you. It's too risky. We can't trust you, so maybe we ought not to even consider your bid as responsive. We'll look at somebody else." That would be a subleverage for Carla to convince her management or partners to up the ante.

Denna:

There's something hidden in this area of cost-plus consulting. What is the underlying premise that supports this type of an arrangement? It is effort. It is good faith effort on the part of both the consultant and those being consulted. Otherwise, that particular arrangement can be very, very costly to both those being consulted and the consultant. There's an implied intent that everything is above board and everyone is going to be looking each other in the eye and proceed forward in good faith.

Aside from hindsight, what should Carla do now? Assume that while the bid was being prepared Carla had these notions inside and said, "Well, I guess he knows what he's talking about" or "I guess I just don't feel I can press it that much." But now, all of her hidden concerns have been confirmed and the partner is doing what she suspected would happen. Now what does she do?

Comment:

She ought to be in a better position now to recognize how important she is to the project; recognizing that gives her tremendous strength. From there, the first problem she has is the question of whether she uses the knowledge that she signed secrecy agreements not to reveal.

And she has to be firm. She has the power to stand up for it, and if she doesn't, she has much to lose in terms of her ability to ever market herself.

It would seem at this point, when her fears are confirmed, that she should insist with her partner that they get back with the client and disclose these alterations in good faith. To do anything less would seem to be hiding further detection down the road; revealing her failure to bring up the issues and insist upon them in the first place.

Denna:

What if the partner continues to insist Carla disclose confidential information to fulfill his promise to the client?

Comment:

If there's pressure on her to disclose confidential information, Carla has a legal, moral, and ethical responsibility to resign; she signed contracts to that effect. The problem that we face as professionals is that the majority of our saleable product is our experience. That's what we have to sell. What we have to offer is our experience, and people are chosen to provide services because of their expertise. Now she has an expertise, and surely, she should be able to draw on the things that she's learned and developed in the past. What she can't do is cross over that line. But it's still her knowledge that's the saleable product by this firm to WGIS.

Comment:

I think it's unfortunate that we get in those binds by definition rather than content. I've been in many situations where I've gone into one company after having been in another and you simply can't suppress what you know. What you don't do is reveal the details of another company, their competitor. You can't say, "Proctor and Gamble is doing it this way," but you have to bring credit. You don't tell people what some particular competitor is doing, but you still use your skill and that's where the power comes from.

Comment:

Keep in mind that the client is insisting on the features of the competition's systems; that's a little bit different than know-how and points out an interesting peculiarity about information systems consulting. You are required to deliver a product, not simply talk about how others are doing things. That's quite different from saying, "Well, here's an alternative that I've seen in other places." The problem that we have in information systems consulting is that you actually deliver something that you can turn on and use and it's not dependent upon someone's expertise. It's simply dependent upon you having a piece of hardware to run a program. This is different from general management consulting when you're talking about marketing ideas or financing ideas. You're actually delivering a product.

Denna:

Just to summarize thus far, one of Carla's alternatives is to forget the whole thing happened, get on with the engagement, and be done with it. The risks would be someone actually taking her to task on the confidentiality agreement that she signed. Another alternative would be to approach the partner and say, "I think we've got to be up front with these people and tell them what's going on," and assume that there's good faith on the part of the client. A third would be to say, "I'm sorry, I'm done," and walk away from it.

Comment:

I think if she's this good, the partner would make some kind of amends to keep her, whether it's a negotiation between the two of them or a negotiation between her and the contract company, WGIS.

Comment:

When you're setting up a system, hardware is universal and anybody can buy it. On the other hand, software may have to be rewritten. Why not take a combination of all that she's learned and put together a new system? The combination can be unique.

Comment:

Recently, a similar suit involving this very issue emerged between Hewlett Packard and Apple Computer. An interface was being delivered and Apple felt they had proprietary rights to it. Although there was a completely different developing team, a completely different product, and a completely different code, at the front end it looked nearly identical. It's the same issue here. We may be able to reverse engineer a project but the idea and the deliverable product are the aspects used for comparison. And at the lowest level there's no difference between any set of computers; it's all zeros and ones. The issue then centers on how they are used.

Denna:

Do you feel uncomfortable with the behavior of the partner? Would you be willing to confront the managing partner? It's a somewhat dangerous path to take, isn't it? No more dangerous than some of the others. In fact, it may be less dangerous than going to jail.

Comment:

Unfortunately, many details are left unknown and some specific actions are going to depend on the environment in which you're in. For example, is the senior partner putting pressure on the partner? If he is, maybe you shouldn't go to that senior partner.

Denna:

What are the specific moral issues that confront Carla, the partner, and the client?

Comment:

Honest estimations, especially in a cost-plus situation. The whole foundation of that very practice is up front integrity on the part of all parties: those supervising the bidding process, those developing the bid, and those receiving the bid.

Comment:

Determining what constitutes proprietary information to the retail industry as well as to a retail information systems specialist is also a moral issue.

Comment:

Another ethical issue is the management of supervisor/labor relationships in skilled professions. Again, that's founded upon the principle that everyone will be open with each other. There's no hidden agenda.

Denna:

At the conclusion of this case what are other ethical issues in the practice of management consulting that are not addressed?

Comment:

Aside from the partner and Carla, you also have to measure moral intent of the firm that's contracting for the services. Do they have a hidden agenda to steal the proprietary information by way of hiring Carla?

Comment:

In the case it appears that they did have an ulterior motive. If someone is underbidding, most entities are smart enough to figure that out, especially if a similar assignment has been done before. In fact, there might have been complicity in agreeing to an unrealistic figure on the part of both WGIS and the people who got the contract — both of them intending to undermine the project with hidden agendas.

Conclusion

Denna:

The issues are endless, and there is no better arena in which an individual can develop a set of moral values than exists in management consulting because it's demanded. For those interested in a long time, long run career in this area, they have to develop a set of moral standards early on, the sooner the better. Such standards do as much to ensure or enhance one's career in this area as just about anything else. You become that much more reliable as a usable resource to a company, and in this area, at least to this point, there are no rules really. There is no code of ethics for systems people, and there's not really one for management consultants in general. If there is one area where we're dependent upon the moral integrity of individuals rather than some governing body, it's management consulting.

Questions

1. Carla has a difficult decision to make. Would her decision have been easier if it had been made in the beginning? How has Carla limited her options?
2. Would Carla have been better off if she would have based her judgements upon her beliefs? Is she partly to blame for the position that she is in?
3. Who has been the most unethical: the partner, Carla, or the client? Do different levels of unethical conduct exist?

11
Ethical Issues for Accountants in Industry___

DANIEL R. COULSON

Mr. Coulson received his bachelor's degree in finance and his MBA from Michigan State University. Currently, he is accounting director for Ford Motor Company's Finance Staff. Since 1965 he has held various analytical and supervisory positions with Ford.

Introduction

Ethics are important to all of us — in business, government, education, and our personal lives. Integrity and ethics are particularly relevant in today's business environment. We continue to hear for example how security law violations and other unethical — and sometimes illegal – behavior within the investment community has shaken Wall Street. The Federal Government also is struggling with ethical issues, both in Congress and the Executive Branch. President Bush, in one of his first official acts, created an ethics commission to monitor the behavior of his top White House and Cabinet officials.

In the business environment, ethics do not just apply to certain segments of business such as defense contractors or the public accounting profession. Ethics are an integral part of our free enterprise system. As part of this system, accountants have a special role and set of responsibilities.

In this chapter, I will be fairly specific. I will describe how we at Ford address the issue of ethics, both in accounting and throughout the company. In doing so, I will describe several real-life examples to illustrate the need *for* and importance *of* ethical behavior. I believe these situations are broadly representative of the kinds of challenges that *all* businesses face on a daily basis.

Accounting and Ethics

Accounting is a set of theories, practices, and procedures for collecting and reporting useful information about the activities and objec-

---

tives of an organization. Although this definition is very broad, it includes an essential element that illustrates the importance of ethics to accounting: this element is the word *useful*. In its broadest sense, useful information is informative, accurate, complete, and timely. It is developed in a consistent way in line with established rules and procedures. It is disclosed clearly and broadly to all who need the knowledge which it provides. In short, it is information that can be relied upon — so that users can understand past results or make decisions about future developments.

Useful also implies a sense of reliability. It is integrity in the accounting process and in the application of accounting standards that produces meaningful results whether these results are viewed as good news or bad by those interpreting the data. Accountants have a responsibility to ensure that their work is guided by this principle. But accountants cannot shoulder this responsibility alone. Ethics must be a guiding principle throughout an organization. It is *not* enough to have good intentions in the accounting area if other functions do not consider ethical behavior essential.

To ensure that ethics receive appropriate attention throughout an organization, the tone must be set at the top. This tone must be consistent in facing all issues and communicated throughout the organization. If this is done, the accountant's job is much easier; he or she is given clear direction to do what is right.

The tone of a company's business conduct is evident in its relations with customers, suppliers, employees, shareholders, and the public. The success of these business relationships is what establishes a company's reputation. In turn, a company's reputation helps determine whether people buy its products, invest in its stock, or become employees. A positive and ethical reputation can give a company a strategic advantage in its business.

Ford's Approach

Ford addresses the issue of ethical behavior directly and in a variety of ways. I'd like to describe some of them to you. First, and perhaps most important, is our environment or corporate culture. Ford is a highly visible, large, multinational company that produces and sells products most people can identify with. Further, Ford has evolved from a "family" business with an historic tradition that is well known throughout the world. This sense of family identity and strong leadership has led Ford to become a "control-oriented" company and one that has been careful to avoid even the perception of wrongdoing in its business practices. This philosophy is *fundamental* to all of our business decisions.

To ensure that this philosophy is understood and applied consistently throughout the company, we have had a Corporate Code of

Conduct for many years. This Code outlines general guidelines to govern the conduct of *all* employees in their internal activities and outside business relationships. Each member of management is responsible for conducting job-related activities in a manner that protects and enhances the company's reputation. Further, management is responsible for informing team members of this policy and to teach by example the exercise of sound and ethical judgment in business relationships.

We also have a strong Audit Committee that is comprised of outside Board members and is responsible for ensuring that management fulfills its responsibilities in preparing financial statements and in maintaining appropriate financial controls.

Ford has formalized policies and procedures for each major function to assist in managing the business. These procedures are published in manuals that address responsibilities and provide guidelines to ensure consistent application throughout the Company.

Like other companies, Ford looks to its public accounting firm, Coopers and Lybrand, to supplement the process for monitoring accounting integrity and internal control. This is especially important in less direct association with Ford's management and environment. We also have an active *internal* audit staff that reviews compliance with our policy manuals and sound business practices. The general auditor reports directly to the chief financial officer and meets privately with the Audit Committee on a regular basis. This helps to ensure the independent status of the internal audit function.

This formalized structure consisting of a Code of Conduct, an Audit Committee, written policies, and external and internal auditors is very helpful but it is *not* sufficient to ensure proper behavior. No set of rules can cover all contingencies and no system of policing can detect all violations. A company, like a community or nation, depends more on the conscience of individuals than on the strictness of law. Corporate ethics, therefore, begin and end with individuals. It is a matter of individual awareness, integrity, and commitment. That is why the selection and development of people is important. We are dependent on quality people with high standards, who want to do the job right, who are concerned about their reputation, *and* who are capable of serving in leadership roles.

When Ford emerged from the recession in the early 1980s, it recognized the need to define better the ideals it stood for and was striving to achieve. As a result, a statement of the Company's Mission, Values, and Guiding Principles (or MVGP as we refer to it) was developed to provide a clear, concise expression of our Corporate objectives: what we stand for, what our priorities are, and how we operate. The MVGP has been distributed to and discussed with all employees. It serves continually to remind us of the Company's purpose.

One of the six Guiding Principles included in the MVGP is our commitment to integrity and high ethical standards. Simply stated, this principle says, "Integrity is never compromised." This sets the tone for ethical behavior throughout the Company in all areas of our business.

Specific Examples of Ethical Accounting Issues

It is essential to have the proper environment to encourage ethical behavior and to have procedures and policies to provide guidance for specific situations. Despite this supportive framework, an accountant, through the nature of his or her responsibilities, faces many situations where professional integrity is required. I would like to describe some of these situations using several examples from our experience at Ford to elaborate.

In describing these, I will cover four separate types of situations:

- those involving ongoing decision-making;

- those connected with implementation of efficiency actions;

- those associated with the process of evaluating and adopting new accounting standards, and, finally;

- the effect of external pressures for improved integrity in financial reporting.

In Ongoing Decision-Making

In our day-to-day work we are often required to make decisions on accounting matters that have ethical implications. The most obvious of these decisions involves the matter and timing with which business transactions are recorded in the financial statements.

- Determining whether it is appropriate to record an event and establish an accrual is an example of this type of situation. Losses associated with closing a facility, for example, often involve difficult decisions regarding the amount of the loss and when it should be recorded. Recognizing contingent liabilities or potential soil cleanup costs are similar kinds of issues.

- Another issue that accountants have to face involves whether a transaction should be capitalized or expensed. Replacing office furniture, for example, can appropriately be capitalized in some situations and expensed in others; the accountant is often required to make this determination.

- A third example that occurs frequently involves the fact that accrual accounting requires recognition of events before all information is known. Accruals for warranty and policy claims, product liability costs, and product obsolescence all involve estimates that rely on the knowledge and integrity of accountants.

Similar kinds of decisions are experienced by all companies and can have an important impact on the financial performance of an operation or an entire company. There can be considerable pressure to overlook the substance of a transaction or to view it from the most optimistic perspective. These pressures must be resisted by all members of management and particularly by controllers and accountants who have a responsibility to evaluate and record events in an unbiased way.

You may have read a recent article in *Fortune* magazine entitled, "Cute Tricks on the Bottom Line." The author of this article believes that "honesty in financial reporting is at an all time low" and that "with so many managers...obscuring the truth, getting to the bottom of the bottom line is more difficult than ever." Some of the common abuses noted in the article were:

- Smoothing quarterly profits by setting up a special reserve rather than reporting a large one-time gain.

- Recording bad news in a single quarter to get it behind you or blame the bad news on the old management.

- Delaying recognition of expenses by recording them at a more opportune time.

- Reducing inventories when profits start to flatten by continuing to ship products even though customers have stockpiles.

- Accelerating or decelerating the write down of assets to produce changes in depreciation expense levels.

- Combining substantial nonrecurring transactions with normal operating results.[1]

I am not sure how frequently these abuses occur in business, but it is important to be aware of these kinds of actions and recognize that they cannot be permitted. Accounting rules allow a certain amount of judgment and flexibility. This must not be abused when reporting financial results. It is the controller's and accountant's responsibility to ensure that integrity and consistency in financial reporting are maintained.

---

[1] Gary Hector, "Cute Tricks on the Bottom Line," *Fortune*, April 24, 1989, pp. 193-200.

While Implementing Efficiency Actions

Accountants also face ethical issues in other, more subtle ways. Here I would like to use an example from my experience at Ford.

For some time, we have been evaluating our business practices within the Company in an attempt to improve them. In accounting this has generally resulted in simpler procedures and controls, more automated systems, and gradual consolidation of organizations and functions. While this has been taking place, the accountant's role has been changing. Clerical handling of data is increasingly being automated or eliminated altogether. Accounting is relinquishing responsibility of certain data to nonaccounting activities, and accounting is doing much less "policing" or double-checking than in the past.

These developments all have ethical implications. Although accounting's role is changing, it cannot relinquish its responsibility for data integrity and the need to report useful information. This means accountants must participate in each of these process improvements to ensure that they give proper recognition to ongoing requirements. This is not to infer that controls cannot be changed; rather, it means change needs to be managed. Alternative or simpler controls and procedures need to be devised and responsibility, when transferred, needs to be clear. To proceed in any other manner would be irresponsible and, in a sense, unethical.

I would like to describe a process improvement made at Ford involving payments for materials purchased from outside suppliers. During the last several years, we've launched a system that allows suppliers to be paid without using invoices. Prior to this, paying a bill required a three-way match: an invoice, with a purchase order, with a receiving document. This matching process added no value to the transaction, but it did serve as a check on the accuracy of the purchasing, receiving, and supplier billing functions. Consequently, it provided comfort to controllers that payments were being made properly.

We now rely on our suppliers and our internal purchasing and receiving activities for *accurate* receipts and *up-to-date* prices. This is supplemented by a system of controls that is incorporated directly in our computer systems. Suppliers receive payment automatically when their shipments are confirmed by our receiving locations and priced by computer price files. No invoices are issued or processed and problems are resolved directly by receiving or purchasing — the activities that have the most knowledge to deal with them. The reliance on other activities, implicit under this new process, depends on responsible and ethical conduct throughout the organization. The accountant's role is to ensure that the system makes sense, includes appropriate controls, and provides accurate financial data.

This is just one example of how process change has affected the way accountants carry out their responsibilities but there are many others. In all cases, however, change must be managed and data integrity assured.

In Evaluating and Adopting New Accounting Standards

Perhaps the most controversial issue facing accounting these days is how to set accounting standards. During the last several years, the FASB has been criticized by industry as being too conceptual and unresponsive to comments. This has been the subject of position papers, studies by Commissions, and comments by the SEC and Congress. Although I do not intend to comment on this subject, I do want to discuss how accountants are affected by the standard-setting process and how this can involve ethical issues.

Consolidation of Majority-owned Subsidiaries ————————————

FASB Statement 94 was approved in late 1987 for adoption by the end of 1988. It requires companies to consolidate in financial reporting the results of all majority-owned subsidiaries, including nonhomogeneous businesses such as financing or real estate. Ford strongly opposed this standard because we thought readers of financial statements would get worse information when we combined the results of our automotive and financial services businesses.

Despite our opposition, the standard became GAAP and we had to comply. The FASB, however, encouraged experimentation in application, and we considered a variety of reporting approaches. We were determined to develop an approach that would not only *meet* the standard but would also continue to provide useful and meaningful information to readers of our financial statements.

After considerable review, we adopted a "business segment" approach in which the results of our automotive and financial services businesses are shown separately and are consolidated at the total-Company level. This complies fully with the standard and retains, in easy-to-read form, the results and financial ratios of our traditional businesses. We have discussed these statements with security analysts and the news media and have received a positive reaction. The approach also is unique in our industry in that business segment information is included in the basic financial statements and is reported each and every quarter.

The ethical issue here is not the final product that was achieved but the process that was involved. This process started with the responsibility to provide meaningful input to the FASB in its deliberation of the accounting issues. Next, was the responsibility to make the best of a difficult issue and continue to provide useful information. We considered easier alternatives, but we chose to present information in the best way we know how, taking into account the users of the data.

Accounting for Postretirement Benefits Other than Pensions _____

There is another emerging accounting issue that will be far more controversial than Statement 94. This issue is accounting for postretirement benefits other than pensions, on which the FASB published an Exposure Draft several months ago. Postretirement benefits include benefits provided by a company for its retired employees and their dependents; the major benefits are for health care and life insurance.

The proposed accounting change for these benefits is significant, and it seems likely that it could force a major reexamination of health care policies both nationally and by individual companies. In the short run, the proposed changes could encourage employers to cut back health care coverage; in the long run, they could create pressure for national policy changes to control health care inflation or to ration health care services.

Satisfactory resolution of this issue is a major challenge for the entire accounting profession. What is needed is an innovative solution that is consistent with the FASB's conceptual framework and takes into account legitimate concerns being raised by business.

Involvement in Issues _____

Parties having an interest in these and similar issues need to participate in the process. Ford considers this particular issue to be very important, and has participated in an FASB Task Force and a Financial Executives Institute Field Test studying the issue. We will also comment on the Exposure Draft and suggest an alternative accounting approach.

All this may not be a matter of ethics, but, in a larger sense, I believe it is. Ethical behavior is not just doing what is right or following the rules; it also involves helping to establish the rules so that useful and meaningful information will be included as part of the financial results. Ethical behavior also involves a responsibility to be objective and to avoid taking self-serving positions unsupported by accounting theory or practical considerations.

Through External Pressure for Improved Integrity in Financial Reporting and Business Conduct

Accountants often find themselves involved in issues related by governmental agencies, legislation, and auditing standards. A number of highly-publicized business failures in the U.S. in recent years has prompted several governmental groups to examine the role of auditors and to challenge existing corporate governance practices. These efforts have resulted in various recommendations to strengthen audit procedures and increase reporting and responsibility by companies.

For example, the National Commission on Fraudulent Financial Reporting — better known as the Treadway Commission — was established in 1985 to study factors contributing to fraudulent financial reporting and to determine how it could be prevented. The Commission concluded that steps could and should be taken to improve financial reporting practices in the U.S. and made a number of recommendations that apply to public companies, independent accountants, regulators, and educators.

The SEC has begun to follow up on the recommendations made by the Treadway Commission. This already has resulted in a proposal to include a report of management's financial responsibilities in annual reports to stockholders and in the Form 10K.

In 1986, the President's Blue Ribbon Commission on Defense Management (Packard Commission) published a report that spelled out six principles of business conduct that address corporate responsibilities under federal procurement laws. All defense industry companies must pledge to follow these six principles and are required to complete a questionnaire on business ethics and conduct.

In 1988, new demands for an adequate program of internal controls were established by the U.S. Government through an amendment of the Foreign Corrupt Practices Act. Under the amendment, accounting provisions of the Act now obligate a U.S. parent company to use its influence to cause its non-U.S. subsidiaries and affiliates (including minority-owned) to adopt acceptable internal control practices.

Each of these developments are examples of external factors that accountants must be aware of and address in their efforts to improve integrity in financial reporting.

Conclusion

To summarize the main point, there are many ethical issues facing accountants today. Some of the issues are obvious, such as misstating earnings to present more favorable performance. Others are much more subtle, however, and involve issues of professional responsibilities to improve continually the quality of our work.

Ethical standards, even at their strongest, are sometimes a little gray around the edges. Any code of ethics must deal with situations involving several legitimate points of view where there is no clear right or wrong answer. Ideals do not always fit perfectly with reality, and ethical standards do not always provide automatic solutions to difficult questions. But this doesn't mean that dilemmas must be accepted. It means only that "gray area" issues require careful examination and thought and all competing interests be clearly identified and evaluated.

Whatever the issue, the accountant cannot face it alone. There must be a clear message throughout an organization that in all situations ethical behavior is the only behavior that is acceptable.

Questions

1. Is ethical behavior in industries only required from the accountants? How has this been violated in the past?
2. Can all contingencies, problems, or violations be governed by a set of rules? What would be better than rules?
3. Where does corporate ethics begin?
4. With all of the judgment calls that face an accountant on a daily basis, how can you be certain that your decision is best?
5. How would you determine between capitalization and expensing costs? Will it change?
6. Must GAAP be followed in an exact fashion, or are creative liberties allowed as long as the presecribed requirements are achieved?

____12
Ethical Issues in Management Accounting — A Case ____

DR. RICHARD McDERMOTT

Dr. McDermott received his doctoral degree from Oklahoma State University. He is currently the Department Chairman for the School of Accountancy at Weber State University in Ogden, Utah. Dr. McDermott previously taught at Brigham Young University. He has done extensive research in systems development for health care institutions.

Introduction ____

Over the past 10 years McBain Enterprises (ME) has emerged as a leader in the robotics industry. ME is a large corporation based in Korea with an American subsidiary, McBain America (MA), in West Virginia. James McBain started ME while stationed in Korea during the war. The autonomous American subsidiary has achieved status as a Fortune 500 company for the past four years with earnings in excess of $1.5 billion.

John Brown took control of MA as its president two years ago. He comes from a background in electronics manufacturing and has been the single most important factor in the increasing strength of the company. As president, Mr. Brown is the main connection with the home offices in Korea. It is his responsibility to report directly to corporate management on the progress or problems that the subsidiary encounters.

Mike Peterson was hired as the controller of MA five years ago. Mr. Peterson has extensive experience in the industry from working for several other robotics firms. His office is adjacent to Mr. Brown's; Mike is considered a vital part of the management team. He reports directly to the president.

Sharlene Jackson is MA's assistant controller. She graduated with high honors from Ethics University and is respected by her coworkers for her hard work and integrity. She has rapidly ascended to her

Reprinted by permission of Dr. Richard McDermott.

current position and feels that her work speaks for itself. Sharlene was hired shortly after Mr. Peterson and has been an integral part of the financial decision-making process. She is considered the one who would likely replace Mr. Peterson as controller.

Dilemma

During the past year, Mr. Brown has focused on increasing the client base for the firm by entertaining corporate executives all over the United States. He told Mr. Peterson that the home office had approved a relatively large expense account for this type of activity. Of course, Mr. Peterson had no objection but asked that Mr. Brown use the usual expense vouchers in order to keep track of these costs for auditing purposes. The president gave these vouchers to Peterson on a weekly basis for review; the vouchers were then given through Ms. Jackson to the accounting staff for recording. Since Peterson knew best which business expenses would be allowable according to the tax laws, it was his responsibility to categorize these vouchers before giving them to Jackson.

On one occasion, Peterson had questions about some of the items that Brown was submitting as a company expense. When he approached Brown about them, Brown indicated that they were items that the home office considered appropriate. When Peterson asked Brown about some things that appeared to be personal expenses, Brown's reply was that they were part of his compensation package as defined by the home office.

Jackson knew of the questionable expenses turned in by Brown but overlooked them because Peterson said that he had done what was necessary to determine their validity. Though she was still wary about these expenses, she didn't give any further thought to the issue until two weeks ago.

Jackson was taking a late lunch and had taken the elevator down to the terrace parking below the company's offices. When she started her car and tried to turn on her radio, she noticed that it would not turn on. She bent over to look under the dash to see if she could adjust the wires and repair it. At that moment, Brown, returning from lunch with an associate, pulled into his stall just across from where Jackson was working on her radio. She overheard Brown's conversation and was surprised to hear what the two gentlemen had to say. Brown's associate was laughing and said he wished he could get his personal expenses covered by his company the way that Brown had.

Jackson was not sure what she should do about what she had heard. She knew that if she reported this to her controller or the home office she might face the same consequences as a colleague of hers who was "released" for questioning the integrity of his superiors. Loyalty is considered a high priority in this Korea-based firm.

1. What should she do with her new-found information?

2. Should she fear for her job if she comes forward with the information?

3. Is it acceptable and even common in business to run small personal expenses through company expense accounts?

4. What are other ethical issues facing management accountants?

Discussion

McDermott:

To begin, this is a Korean corporation and a Fortune 500 company; within the corporate culture, loyalty plays a major role.

There is an inherent loyalty to the company as well as loyalty to management. Also consider that since the company is based in Korea, it may not have good communications with its employees in the United States. In fact, the president is primarily responsible for communications with the Korean management, but apparently the founder, James McBain, is still in Korea, which causes some communication problems.

The company is in an expansion mode. As a result, Korean management has approved a large entertainment budget for which Mr. Brown is really the main contact person. What then is known about Brown? Is he a successful CEO?

Comment:

The case study indicates that he has been the single most important factor in increasing the strength of the company. Mr. Brown probably has a great deal of credibility with management in Korea. Apparently, he also has quite a bit of autonomy by virtue of the fact that he is in the United States while McBain is in Korea.

McDermott:

Now the controller has apparently questioned the president's entertainment expenses and has been told by the president that these are a part of his compensation.

Comment:

There probably is cheating going on, although it may be that what the president says is true. In fact, he may have an agreement with his boss that much of his personal expenses will be picked up; this may indeed be a part of his compensation package.

Even if that is true, however, there is an ethical problem because taxes are not being withheld on these benefits.

McDermott:

We can examine this case from a couple of levels. We can examine it from a corporate standpoint and an individual standpoint. At what level does the problem exist?

Comment:

Note that practices such as these are not considered inappropriate in countries like Korea. A few years ago, when these practices were revealed, Congress made it illegal. From a corporate standpoint, it is likely that Brown is spending money that is not authorized by Korean management.

McDermott:

One tool to use in analyzing ethics cases is stakeholder analysis. First, identify stakeholders and then show how they are affected by the breech of ethics. Who are the stakeholders in this case?

Comment:

One of them is the assistant controller, Ms. Jackson, who is respected for her hard work and integrity. Because she heard the president's conversation, she is the one who must make the decision. She must ask herself, "Am I being faithful to myself? Do I have as much integrity as others think I have or am I allowing a scam to occur?"

McDermott:

Other stakeholders include: Mike Peterson, Mr. Brown, the Internal Revenue Service, and Corporate Management. But how about the employees who observe the president? How does this affect their behavior? Then there are the stockholders who are also stakeholders. The president's personal expenses paid by the company reduce profits available for their dividends.

Comment:

It is specifically the employees who are greatly affected by a breech of ethics. It has been said that you cannot raise the ethics of an organization; they basically have to filter down from the top. I think that those in top positions have to demonstrate ethics in their own actions.

In fact, the management team has been there longer than the president, and these people are noted for their integrity.

McDermott:

Peterson has gone to the president who has assured him that the expenses in question are approved by Korean management. Was this a satisfactory answer? Does he have an additional obligation to the board or to other stakeholders? What are Peterson's responsibilities?

Perhaps he ought to explain to Brown the risk of his behavior. If he does so, what will be the effect on Brown and what will likely be the effect on Peterson?

Comment:

Unfortunately, Peterson may have to be prepared to look for another place to work. Regardless, he should explain to Brown that he needs documentation for his tax files as well as authorization from the home office. He has the additional option of speaking to the audit committee.

Peterson needs to make it clear to Brown that some of these expenses are compensations and should be recorded as such, rather than as entertainment expenses.

Keep in mind that Peterson hasn't heard of the president's conversation. Jackson is the one on the spot. She has two choices: she can go to Peterson or she can keep quiet. Until she takes action, Peterson doesn't know there is a problem.

Comment:

But we don't know that anything wrong has been done. There have been some innuendoes, but we don't know that Brown has purchased personal items on account. The way the case reads, you don't even really know that what Brown said is not true. All we have is the statement of a friend who says, "I wish I could get my company to pay my personal expenses the way you have." That doesn't say that Brown is doing it dishonestly or without the knowledge of management in Korea. It just says that the company is covering some of Brown's personal expenses. It may be that these expenses are not being treated correctly on the books but they may still be legitimate.

McDermott:

What if Jackson notifies Peterson and he says, as he apparently said in the case, "I have already cleared this with Korean management." Does Jackson have any further responsibilities?

Comment:

One of the things the National Association of Accountants is doing in their discussion of ethical dilemmas for management accountants is to look at the responsibilities of accountants at various levels. I think it is very clear that accountants cannot accept the idea that they should just do what they are told. When necessary, they need to skip organizational levels to see that things are properly solved.

McDermott:

As a matter of fact, a document called "Standards of Ethical Conduct for Management Accountants" addresses this issue. It states, "In applying the standards of ethical conduct, management accountants may encounter problems in identifying unethical behavior and in resolving ethical conflict. When faced with significant ethical issues, management accountants should follow the established policies of the organization bearing on the resolution of such conflict. Management accountants should consider the following courses of action: discuss such problems with the immediate superior except when it appears the superior is involved, in which case the problem should be presented initially to the next higher management level; if satisfactory resolution cannot be achieved when the problem is initially presented, submit the issues to the next higher managerial level; if the immediate superior is the chief executive officer or equivalent the acceptable reviewing authority may be a group such as the audit committee, executive committee, board of directors, board of trustees, or owners. Contact with levels above the immediate superiors should be initiated only with the superior's knowledge."

As mentioned earlier, Peterson should probably talk with Brown first and depending on what happens there, proceed up the organization.

The NAA's statement says that management accountants should, "Clarify relevant concepts by confidential discussion with an objective adviser to obtain an understanding of possible courses of action. If ethical conflicts still exist after exhausting all levels of internal review, the management accountant may have no other recourse on significant matters than to resign from the organization and to submit an informative memorandum to an appropriate representative of the organization."

Comment:

The key words are "significant matters." I don't know that my own individual cost/benefit analysis would tell me to risk my job for the issue of a president turning in some expenses. There is a difference between causing financial statements to be falsified and taking pencils home. Somewhere you've got to make a judgment about significance. This is the real world. You should not throw your position away over something that does not matter.

McDermott:

How much does the issue of materiality play in an ethical issue like this, and how do you decide what is material? What guidelines do you use?

Comment:

You need to consider the stakeholders and determine the resulting damage that was caused. If the stakeholders are the shareholders and the related financial misinterpretation and fraud could seriously harm the people who invest in the company, I might conclude that the problem is significant. I am not sure that turning in country club expenses to a multinational company is significant, however.

Consider also that you could significantly destroy your relationship with the president, which would consequently destroy your ability to be of value to the organization. When you destroy relationships or credibility over a small or insignificant issue, a few hundred dollars, that may not be good judgment. It would be different if it was a multimillion dollar situation.

One of the rationalizations is that, "If I do this I won't have my job any longer. I can protect the stakeholders more by keeping my job."

Comment:

While this may be true, if Jackson didn't say anything to anyone, especially her immediate superior, she really would be of little value when large things came up. If you agree with the smaller compromises, people are not going to listen to you when something bigger comes up. My approach in this case would be to approach Peterson and say, "I heard this conversation and I thought you should be aware of it," and see how things went from there and not resign over something that you heard while your presence was unknown. In any case, I think she should do something.

Comment:

From the standpoint of an internal auditor, I have a great deal of independence and authority within the corporation. If this had happened to one of my people, there wouldn't be any question but that it would be pursued. In principal it is wrong, and we don't want something wrong to be accepted. Those same principles apply to the management accountant. In many companies, unless we ask for it, we are not going to get the kind of status and authority that we need in situations like these. We should have primary responsibility in determining what is acceptable and senior management should not be in the position to overrule us or say, "That is the way I want to do it, forget about the questions you have raised." This philosophy needs to come down from the level of the board of directors and audit committee. Position should not influence behavior. People need to understand that the management accountant has a field of expertise, and they need to pay attention to him as he resolves issues like these. In this case, there is a matter of principle that ought to be pursued.

Unfortunately, we don't have any perception of the materiality of the personal expenses being claimed by the president. Sometimes, however, principles rule regardless of materiality because some small issues establish a precedence. Now if it came to a contest of wills and Peterson said to Jackson, "I've looked at this and it is insignificant.

Maybe we are bending some rules on the taxes but it is no big deal and I think we ought to forget about it." Then she would probably have a pretty good basis for forgetting it. But she needs to raise the issue.

As for her options, as assistant controller she is certainly in a position to pull the file and see if there is any evidence to back up the conversation she overheard. If she approaches Peterson with facts, she is in a much better position than if she just says, "Hey, guess what I heard out in the parking lot."

Comment:

It seems that the bigger question here is how much do you have to agree with or how much of a policeman does a controller have to be? The big picture is that there are some things that you can live with and some things that you can't. In my own mind I am more concerned by what goes into the financial statements. There are certain things that I would simply not live with. Yet, there is a lot that I have admittedly turned my back on given the nature of the circumstances. When I felt things were not material, I have come to the conclusion that the fight was not prudent. Does the controller have to be the company's conscience in all circumstances? I would say no. Certainly in some circumstances he has to be but in others probably not. Granted, controllers in companies that have a good audit committee and have internal auditors have an advantage over controllers who don't.

Comment:

Any time the controller knows of some instance of dishonesty, even small, he has to raise questions about the people involved. Materiality has only to do with how far the issue should be taken.

In an organization, people are given an area of responsibility in which they make judgments. Someone at some time has given Brown the impression that he has a great deal of latitude within which to make judgment calls. Although Jackson still doesn't know whether in fact those expenses are personal, Peterson has a responsibility that is bigger than hers and he says the expenses are valid. Moreover, Brown has an area of responsibility that is bigger than Peterson's and he says they are valid. So Jackson's whole dilemma centers on, "Is this important enough to me to investigate further and move the issue up the ladder or is this something I can forget.

The question is one of documentation. If the president claims that this is part of his compensation package, then Jackson has every right in the world to say, "Well, let's get some documentation." She should pursue it from that angle, otherwise she is taking a real chance of losing her job by doing nothing at all. If the auditors perform an audit and find out that she is not fulfilling her responsibilities, she will likely be replaced.

Comment:

That is something that a good human relations person should be able to handle. I think Peterson should prepare a memo on what is compensation and what is a legitimate expense and forward it to Korea.

Comment:

I'd like to pick up on the fear of losing one's job. We are all worried about our jobs and whether we are doing them right. But in most cases that doesn't become a problem if we handle these situations properly. Often, when someone is claiming personal expenses in an incorrect way, the problem is that the employer does not have a knowledge of the tax rules.

    It is important as the tax advisor to sort out these issues with your employer because if the IRS sees these little errors, you lose your credibility. The IRS will then be inclined to dig deeper and take issue with many things at great cost to the taxpayers. Thus, even if it is a small item, there is reason to pursue it, get it sorted out, get it documented, and agree how you are going to handle it.

Comment:

Worse than being fired in a situation like that described in the case is having your life made miserable by an angry boss. That is why many people don't press an issue like this — they know that they have to live with that person at least 40 hours a week. Ethics are often easier said than done.

    Whistle blowers pay a price for their actions. You may not get fired, but you end up paying the price.

McDermott:

What other ethical issues face management accountants? One issue is knowing one's area of responsibility. In this case, what is Jackson's real realm of responsibility? She overheard a conversation — should she come forth and talk about it?

Comment:

She ought to say something about it, but the whole issue of how she says it, who she says it to, and how far she pushes her views, is one of those nebulous areas that we struggle with. When it comes down to it, it is very difficult for anyone to sit down and say here is the absolute to apply in all situations or even most situations or for all people. In the case of Jackson and the conversation she overheard, you can't take everything you heard at face value. What she overhead might just be a comment that has absolutely nothing to do with her concerns.

We should look at management accountants as two players: an individual accountant and a team player, both with particular relationships to worry about. There has to be give and take. The whole idea of ethical responsibility is an individual choice. It is one that you've got to make early. You have to know where you stand and be able to live with the consequences of your decisions.

Questions

1. Does commonality in business override ethical concerns?
2. In this case, can Jackson consciously ignore the information that he has received? In ethical concerns, should we be concerned about others' actions or should we only be concerned about our own?
3. Should materiality be a factor in determining whether an ethical concern should be ignored?
4. Internal problems can be quite intimidating to young employees. What could the company do to make such problems easier to handle?
5. What controls or precautions are you aware of that companies have used to make it easier for employees to reveal information regarding unethical behavior? Have they been effective?

13
Ethical Issues Facing Young Accountants — The Early Years_____

LOREE DUNN HAGEN

Ms. Hagen graduated from Brigham Young University, as one of the top students, with a master's degree in accounting and was a member of Phi Kappa Phi. She recently moved to the San Francisco office of Price Waterhouse after working two and a half years with Touche Ross & Co. in Washington, D.C.

Introduction _____

Ethics has long been a subject of particular interest to me and a topic of frequent conversation since I started my career almost three years ago. I thought a lot about ethical issues before I finished school in an attempt to prepare myself to act properly when faced with ethical dilemmas at work.

Most of the ethical problems I considered were of the nature of those addressed in the case studies presented in this book. As a fairly new accountant, however, I have found that the types of ethical problems discussed up to this point, although common, are not the only kind of issues facing the new accountant. More specifically, I am referring to situations where the law or the rules of the profession prescribe one course of action and the firm or the client urges you to take another position.

Ethics Defined _____

Before I describe the different kinds of ethical problems that are most often faced by new accountants, I would like to establish a definition of ethics. Defining ethics is very important because some of the problems expressed to me as I have talked with people at various firms and companies, both in and out of public accounting, go beyond the typical discussion of ethics. Hopefully, by establishing a

Reprinted by permission of Loree Dunn Hagen.

broad definition of ethics, you can clearly see how these other problems fit under the ethics umbrella.

Ethics, more than just adherence to a professional code of ethics, is a study of ideal human character, actions, and ends. Ethics is adherence to moral principles, quality, or practice. Morality is characterized by excellence in what pertains to practice or conduct. Morality is sanctioned by one's conscience.

When I finished school, I found I suddenly had time, albeit on mass transit to and from work, to do a lot of reading. To foster my interest in moral philosophy, I read Adam Smith's *Theory of Moral Sentiments* and I have learned to appreciate great masters such as Plato, Aristotle, and Spinoza. When they speak of ethics, their treatises are not outside our realm; their ideas apply fully to each of us in our professional careers.

These masters speak of ethics as positive good, implying that you actually have virtuous, good, positive behavior in any situation in which you find yourself. You should then be a good influence on your community, on your profession, and on your family. Ethics is basically just an adherence to a very high and well thought out set of personal principles and priorities.

Ethical Issues _____

For ease of presentation, I have broken down ethical problems into three basic categories. The first is an area where there is a right answer. These are very real problems with very real pressures but in my opinion there is a right answer. However foggy and difficult to act upon, the right answer does exist.

The second category deals with problems that are much more personal and internal in nature which do not have a single right answer. Such problems cause a little more struggling to find the moral solution. Whether you feel strong enough to carry out the action is another problem.

Unfortunately, the third category occurs all too frequently in the profession. I am referring to the situation where the new accountant feels very strongly about a particular position but is feeling pressure, from either the manager on the job or client pressure passed through the manager or the partner, to take another position. A related issue arises when the new accountant knows or suspects errors in the information or presentation but, again, is too distant from the decision-making process to make an impact.

Issues With A Right Answer

To illustrate these three ideas, I will share some examples. The first category involves issues where there is a right answer. In public accounting, all the profession has to offer is expertise and time. Consequently, charging time is a very important part of the working process for a young accountant. You accomplish little if you do a lot of work for a client and you do not bother charging the time. I am reminded time and again by partners that the accounting business is for profit. We are there to serve clients but there is a profit motive. You have to charge your time.

As simple as that may sound, I am amazed at the struggles that are created for young accountants in trying to figure out just how much time to charge or trying to decide how to charge that time. I had not really anticipated this type of a problem. In any event, the problem arises because there are some cyclical pressures in the business. Although an office may be doing well, there is a pressure to grow or to increase gross services, which is not much more than time charged by the people. Along with this pressure to charge more time, you may even feel a pressure to inflate your time.

Alternatively, as this cycle progresses, the office has difficulty recovering because it takes employees eight hours to finish a six hour job, or partners set fixed fees that are below the actual time charged. As a result, you get opposing pressure to be more careful about the way you charge your time and to be sure you are working efficiently.

The result of these pressures is reflected in the budget that you are given for a job. Suppose you have a big client who typically pays its fees. When the pressure is to charge time, you are given a pretty lenient budget; however, when the pressure changes, the manager in setting that budget makes some changes. He wants to recover all the items he charged to that client. All of a sudden, for the same work you get a much smaller budget and feel pressure to perhaps "eat" some time to fit within that budget.

This is a difficult problem for the young accountant but there is a right answer. If you have spent good time on the client, then you should charge the time to the client. If you have not spent good time on the client, then you should not charge the time. Although this answer seems fairly cut and dry, in actuality it is a daily crisis for most new accountants. Part of the problem is remembering exactly what you did throughout the day, but there is also the pressure of determining if time spent was really good time. This is a real dilemma that the new accountant needs to consider before the issue arises.

Issues With More Than One Right Answer

The second category may be slightly out of the mainstream, but I have talked to other young accountants in various firms around the country and they have echoed the following concerns. This area has been a problem on an individual basis, and the firm may not even realize the intensity of the situation. In fact, most people I have seen leave the profession have left because of the kind of struggles I am going to describe. The personal pressure becomes too great, the problem goes unresolved, and people leave public accounting to find something a little less demanding. This area covers problems primarily of conflicting commitments — feeling strongly about one set of priorities but living another.

The best way to describe this situation is to share a personal experience. When my fiance proposed, we decided to have a two week period of understanding before we told anybody that we were engaged. This was a time to bring skeletons out of the closet and discuss any problems we thought we might have that could be a problem in our marriage.

During this time, I remember telling him that one of my greatest concerns was his career. He is an attorney, and I am well aware of the kind of hours attorneys work and the career path that they pursue. I said, "I want you to understand now that I do not want to marry a paycheck. I do not need to marry a paycheck. I make good money on my own, and unless I can feel assured that I will be able to see you on a regular basis, it will be a problem for me."

He was able to make this commitment. He has held up his end of the bargain; he is home quite a bit. Unfortunately, I have not been there. I feel very strongly that I should spend time at home and on other commitments, but work pressures get quite heavy sometimes. There are deadlines to be kept, and there are client needs to be met on a moment's notice. I do not think in three years time that I have once been able to tell anyone what time I was going to show up anywhere. I feel like I have been living on an "if nothing happens I will be there" premise for the past two and a half years. Not surprisingly, I am not the only one that has felt that pressure; everyone I spoke with expressed similar concerns.

One fellow who is in tax said he has not seen his children since January because they are in bed before he gets home. This is something we in public accounting need to recognize as an ethical dilemma.

Some pressures in this area arise, again, because accounting is a business for profit and there is a very steep pyramid. You must work hard and be career oriented to continue moving up the ladder. If you work a 12 to 14 hour day, however, there is not much time left for any other activities.

There are also what I call "artificial deadlines" from time to time. In tax, we have very real deadlines — the 15th of almost every month. But there are other deadlines where a manager or partner would like to look at something tomorrow, and the new accountant feels a strong pressure to meet that deadline. Obviously, one might be a little hesitant to say, "I really needed to have some time. I am involved in the Jaycees or Kiwanis and I have made a commitment to be there this evening."

I have finally gotten brave about speaking up, and, for the most part, I have found that it has not created any problem. The manager will tell you if the deadline is critical and then you have to evaluate your priorities. On the other hand, there are times when the deadlines are not very real, and I think it is important that new accountants realize that some requests can be adjusted.

Ask yourself if these are really ethical dilemmas. In our earlier broad definition of ethics, if you are feeling the struggle at the very core of your personal values, then it is definitely an ethical question.

Issues That Involve Pressures

The third category consists of typical ethical problems. These are the issues that I had thought about before working and which are discussed frequently, but they are probably the most embarrassing for the profession and the ones that a new accountant is least empowered to do anything forceful about. In order to illustrate what a new accountant goes through, I am going to share some specific examples that come from a variety of firms.

One common situation lies in the recent tax legislation. Congress has significantly tightened up on the losses you can take from passive activities. Included in the law is a stiff hourly participation requirement by people involved in passive investments. Instead of asking the client how many hours a week or month are devoted to passive income items, the accountant will tell a client what is required to recognize the loss. The client can then reevaluate the hours, possibly by including time spent thinking about the passive activity in the car or at home. Somehow the client manages to meet the hourly requirement and this puts the new accountant in a tight situation. You may feel like it is wrong, but there is a real question as to what you can really do to resolve the situation.

The second example focuses on a young accountant who has a knowledge or a strong suspicion of false representations made by a client. A very wealthy man loaned his brother $600,000. This loan was not a material item for him and for loan purposes there was nothing in writing, there was no rate established, and there was no evidence of ability to repay. The ability to repay, however, was not likely. The brother made no attempt to collect on the loan, and, at tax preparation time, it was written off as a bad debt loss. Granted, the brother would like to take the loss, but, in fact, it was a gift.

The situation arose when the new accountant said, "This looks like a gift to me. I cannot classify this as a loss." The higher management person replied, "I have promised the client that he will receive the deduction," and the discussion was over. These issues are faced by the new person, and the question then becomes, what can a new person do? Before you reach management level, you really are not empowered in the decision process.

To address this dilemma, the new person must first voice disagreement to her superiors. In a clear ethical situation you should not feel uncomfortable in going as high as partner level, if need be. You don't have to just sit there and brood about these problems. Don't assume that they could not be persuaded or at least benefitted by hearing your objections.

Conclusion

We all need to assess where our loyalties lie and how we are going to handle ethical situations. I have no concrete answer to this group of problems; however, it will be a sad day when we stop talking about them and stop trying to struggle through the alternatives to avoid these kinds of problems in the future.

As established at the outset, ethics, morals, virtue, and excellence can all be considered in the same family. In light of this statement, consider this brief quote from Aristotle:

> *We do not act rightly because we have virtue or excellence, but we rather have these because we have acted rightly. These virtues are formed in man by his doing the actions.*

Questions

1. Have you decided how you will handle your future ethical problems? What can you do now to make future concerns easier to handle?
2. What problems do you think you will be faced with as a new employee in the business world?

14
Ethical Issues Facing New Accountants — The Later Period

L. SCOTT HOBSON

Mr. Hobson graduated, as one of the top students from Brigham Young University, with a master's degree in accountancy in 1983. He is currently a consulting manager with Price Waterhouse in San Jose. His specialties include rate management and regulatory issue skills, financial planning and control, and small-scale systems.

Introduction

As mentioned in the introduction of this book, three factors — common in incidences of fraud — might also have application in ethical situations. In his introduction, Dr. Albrecht explained that:

- First, there must be some **pressure**, financial or otherwise, on the individual.

- Second, there must be an **opportunity** to do something fraudulent.

- Third, the individual must be able to **rationalize** what he or she has done.

I would like to present my observations on ethical issues facing new accountants in light of these three factors.

Because I have worked for Price Waterhouse for five and a half years, my observations are based primarily upon my public accounting experience, although I believe the same kinds of issues would apply to young accountants in industry as well.

Primary Concerns

I believe that all new accountants have two primary concerns when they obtain their first job. The first concern is their own performance.

Reprinted by permission of L. Scott Hobson.

They must perform at the standards established by the firm as well as their personal standards. The second concern is a desire to advance within the firm as quickly as possible. These concerns result in pressure, real or perceived, that could lead a young accountant to commit some act in violation of his professional or personal code of ethics.

Performance Measurement

Since advancement is primarily dependent on one's performance as a new accountant, it might be useful to focus on how performance is measured. A new accountant is evaluated on two primary factors: chargeability and work quality.

Chargeability

The first factor is chargeability. That is, how many of the 2,080 available hours in a normal work year were spent on client projects? Entry-level staff are expected to be chargeable between 1,700 and 1,900 hours per year. They are evaluated at the end of each year on whether or not they have met their target for chargeable hours.

The need to maintain a high level of chargeability puts pressure on staff accountants, leading some to perform in an unethical manner. For example, staff accountants must account for eight hours per day on their time sheets. Occasionally, however, if staff in the office are not assigned to a particular project, they leave for home about 3:00 or 3:30 in the afternoon. The two hours spent out of the office are generally charged to some administrative code.

Occasionally, there is pressure not to charge hours actually worked. For example, most businesses tend to experience cycles or periods of high activity followed by periods of low activity. My office is no exception. At various times during the last five years, the managing partner directed that no overtime was permitted without prior partner approval. Such instructions result from a concern that there were some staff members who were not being utilized fully and others that were working a tremendous amount of overtime. The "no overtime" policy was intended to even out the workload by using available staff on difficult engagements.

Practically, though, on jobs where there is a fairly short report deadline or particularly difficult accounting transactions to be tested, the manager or the senior would say, "We are going to have to work the hours required, but since we are not allowed to work overtime, just reflect eight hours a day on your time sheet." I believe that most young accountants have been asked not to charge the actual time worked on specific projects.

Work Quality

The second evaluation factor is work quality. Did you produce a good work product? Were you accurate? Did you complete your work in a timely manner? Did you keep your supervisor or senior informed of issues as they arose in the course of your work so that there were no surprises at the end of the engagement?

The need to produce a quality product within a limited budget may put pressure on some accountants to compromise their ethical standards. For example, after a report has been issued or earnings have been released, some clean-up work is still required in preparing the workpapers for final review and sign-off. During that time, a staff accountant may occasionally come across an error that either he made or, if he is in a position to review someone else's workpapers, that they have made. There may be pressure at that point not to report the error to anyone.

Another situation young accountants may face arises when they are responsible for some detailed testing that must be completed within a certain budget. In testing accounts payable, a staff accountant may look at invoices and make sure that there is proper support and proper approval. If he is under a significant time constraint and has drawn a random sample of fifty items, he may be tempted to look at forty or forty-five of them and say, "Well, these forty-five have been fine; the other five must be fine too" and conclude on that basis.

Another situation may occur at the end of a project, when the senior or manager has reviewed the workpapers and prepared a list of review points that the staff accountant is responsible to clear. If the budget has already been exceeded, there may be a temptation to claim that he has followed up on a particular point when he has not.

Another issue having to do with work quality that is not quite as clear cut in terms of what is ethical, is in the area of expertise. I had an experience where I was repeating on an audit client for the second year. The senior assigned to the client was rescheduled to another client due to scheduling conflicts, leaving me in charge of the project after just over one year's experience with the firm. This meant that I was not only responsible for performing certain testing of sections for the first time but also reviewing work that had been done by others. Frankly, I felt very unprepared to handle the responsibility.

In these situations, some accountants may feel that if they hesitate or refuse to perform, they are jeopardizing their advancement or future assignments in the firm. There exists some pressure when work you are not really prepared to do gets pushed down to your level.

Other Issues

Another issue has to do with confidential information obtained through client assignments. For example, I am the project manager of a world-wide semiconductor industry survey. We are an independent third party that collects sales and order information from participating companies. With this information, we publish a report that is closely watched by the high tech stock market as a barometer of the health of the semiconductor industry. The data that we collect and publish is highly sensitive. Occasionally, I receive pressure from individuals, both inside and outside Price Waterhouse, who would like to have access to that information to help them assess the health of a particular company. Obviously, I have an ethical responsibility to protect the confidentiality of the data.

Finally, let me briefly address an administrative issue–expense reports. For most new accountants, the public accounting job will provide the first experience they have with an expense account. Staff have the opportunity to charge work-related expenses that they incur either to a client or to the firm. Some accountants are tempted to charge personal expenses to clients or their firm without proper documentation.

For example, Price Waterhouse's policy used to be that if you worked ten hours in any one day, you were allowed an overtime per diem of $11. Some individuals have mentioned that they did very well with the overtime per diem because, if they worked twelve hours in one day and eight hours in another day, they would shift two hours to the second day so that they could charge the per diem allowance on both days.

Conclusions and Recommendations

Many different pressures exist for new accountants resulting primarily from their desire to perform and advance within their firm. Opportunities to commit unethical acts are available in the public accounting environment, and many young accountants are skilled at rationalizing their actions.

In closing, I would like to offer some suggestions for similar situations that may be faced by new accountants. First, you should work out your response ahead of time. Situations are not always black and white; there are many gray areas. If you have worked out your response ahead of time and know how you want to react to these situations, you don't need to make your decision under the pressure of the situation.

Second, the most important thing you can do to get help when faced with a difficult issue is to pick a mentor. Your mentor should be someone you can trust; someone you can go to and talk through the situation. In our firm, we are assigned both partner and manager-mentor relationships. Every staff has regular staff evaluations with a specific partner and manager. During these meetings, they are invited to bring up any issues that might be troubling them. I find these meetings to be a little too formal. I suggest that you are much better off picking someone with whom you are comfortable as an informal mentor. You should visit them on an informal basis when something is troubling you.

Finally, I think Shakespeare said it best when he said, "To thine own self be true and it must follow as the night the day, thou canst not then be false to any man." I believe that if you will use that philosophy as your personal code of ethics you will make the right choices when faced with the kinds of situations I have described and always be on the ethical side of the issue.

Questions

1. What kind of pressures do new accountants face? What can be done to eliminate these pressures in personal areas, in educational areas, and in vocational areas?
2. What problems can pressure, opportunity, and rationalization create in accounting?
3. Why should we work out some answers to ethical concerns ahead of time?

15
Ethical Issues for
Young Accountants —
A Case

DR. JIM D. STICE

Dr. Stice received his doctoral degree from the University of Washington. He is currently an Assistant Professor in the School of Accountancy at Brigham Young University. Dr. Stice previously taught at the University of Washington.

Introduction

You are a staff accountant on the audit of Meadow Creek Furniture Manufacturing Company. The company has been in existence for twenty years and employs 200 people in Tupelo, Mississippi — a town of 30,000 people. At the time of the audit, the national economy is at the peak of a recessionary period. The furniture industry as a whole is very adversely affected by recessions. Not surprisingly, Meadow Creek is experiencing some serious financial difficulties.

During the conduct of the audit, you discovered evidence that makes you believe that the going concern assumption is in serious doubt. You feel that Meadow Creek's ability to survive the recession is questionable.

The company is privately held with 50 percent of the stock or $500,000 held by the founder and president, Bill McKay. The remaining $500,000 is held by ten of Bill's friends and acquaintances. If the company is forced to liquidate, the stockholders will most likely lose 90 percent of their investment.

The company needs financing. Bill, however, does not want to sell more stock because he is aware of the company's precarious financial condition and does not want to involve any other friends in the business. In order to obtain financing, Bill has applied for a $500,000 loan with First Commercial Bank.

Reprinted by permission of Dr. Jim D. Stice.

Dilemma _____

If Meadow Creek does not receive the loan, or some other type of financing, the business will be forced to liquidate. Even if Bill does receive the loan, you believe the continuing existence of meadow Creek is questionable. Furthermore, if the business is forced to liquidate, Bill will lose his entire investment. The stockholders will also suffer substantial losses. As the staff auditor, you recognize that issuing a qualified opinion regarding the going concern of Meadow Creek Company could result in the company's not receiving the financing needed. On the other hand, if your firm does not mention the going concern issue, the bank makes the loan, and Meadow Creek goes bankrupt, you may be sued by the bank for the $500,000.

Significant Audit Discoveries

Your observation of the physical inventory revealed that inventory recorded on the books at $100,000 consisted of outdated and obsolete styles. An independent sales organization estimated that the inventory could probably be sold for $50,000. Bill, however, refuses to write down the inventory, insisting that it will be sold for at least $100,000 after the recession "blows over."

Also included in inventory is $50,000 of merchandise sold to, and on the premises of, Rainbow Furniture Company. Currently, Rainbow is in bankruptcy and is expected to pay creditors $.10 on the dollar. No consignment agreement exists; nevertheless, Bill claims title to the goods in lieu of the $50,000 receivable due from Rainbow. No bad debt has been recorded. Bill has even suggested that they might drive a truck over to Rainbow and forcibly retrieve the merchandise.

Art Vance, an obese customer who purchased one of Meadow Creek's sofas in Michigan, is suing Meadow Creek for damages incurred while sitting down on the sofa. Mr. Vance alleges that he sat down on the sofa and the springs were of insufficient strength and quality to support his weight, thereby causing a permanent back injury. Mr. Vance claims that he has suffered physical pain, has missed work, and has experienced emotional distress as a result of the injury and is suing Meadow Creek for $500,000. Competent legal counsel to Meadow Creek has asserted that the probability is about 50 percent that Meadow Creek will lose an estimated $100,000. This contingent liability has not been recorded in the financial statements nor disclosed in the footnotes.

Prior to the Meadow Creek audit, you had worked on the audit of Universal Furniture Company, a major furniture retailer. During the course of the audit, you discovered that a bill received from Meadow Creek Furniture Company for goods shipped costing $82,000 had been billed to Universal for only $28,000. Catching the error,

Universal considered it their good fortune and gladly submitted payment for $28,000. Subsequently, they received a statement from Meadow Creek indicating payment received in full.

As auditor, you had requested that Universal submit the deficient payment and record the corresponding liability. Universal recorded the liability but was unwilling to submit payment. You requested permission to notify Meadow Creek Company of the erroneous bill; however, Universal management denied your request. Obviously, Meadow Creek is in dire need of the $54,000 payment that Universal still owes.

The senior and manager on the engagement are concerned that the inclusion in the financial statements of all the items discovered during the course of the audit may seriously jeopardize Meadow Creek's receipt of the loan. Without the loan, the company's survival is not likely. In addition, 200 people will lose their jobs in a community where the unemployment rate is already much higher than the national average.

You believe that Generally Accepted Auditing Standards require that the going concern issue be disclosed in the opinion. The senior and manager, however, are inclined to accept the company's representations and issue a clean opinion. They believe that if Meadow Creek receives the loan, they will probably be able to repay the loan, especially if the recession ends early, but there is nothing concrete in the financial statements to support that opinion.

1. Should you accept the senior's and manager's position and go along with the clean opinion? If not, what should you do?

2. Should your firm inform Meadow Creek of the underbilling to Universal?

3. How far should a staff accountant go in pushing his or her opinions?

4. What are other ethical issues facing young accountants?

Case Background

Stice:

In analyzing the case, assume the role of a staff auditor. You are the low man on the totem pole. Now, during the audit, you come upon a couple of matters that raise concern. First, there is obsolete inventory valued on the books at $100,000. An independent service says it is only worth $50,000, yet Mr. McKay says he will not write it down. He says that when the recession blows over he will get at least $100,000 for it.

Second, a bad debt exists. Meadow Creek sold $50,000 worth of merchandise to a company that is now expected to pay $.10 on the dollar. But Bill insists that he is going to run over there with a truck and get it, if need be. So, he is not willing to write that off as bed debt.

A third item discovered in the course of the audit was a contingent holding. A rather large man sat on a couch, the couch broke, he suffered damages and is suing Meadow Creek for $500,000. The attorneys say there is a 50 percent chance of losing $100,000, yet Bill McKay is not willing to disclose that either.

Lastly, there is a receivable that presents a major concern. Your firm audits a customer of Meadow Creek. Meadow Creek sold the customer goods for a price of $82,000 and subsequently billed them for only $28,000. Universal is the company. The staff accountant on the audit of Universal discovered the error and asked Universal to pay the full amount, but they refused. First, what can be done about the receivable? Can you tell Meadow Creek? What is required of Universal?

As it is presented in the case, the audit firm basically has two options. They can give a clean opinion, in which they may leave themselves wide open for a lawsuit from the bank should this company go under. They can argue that it is not an accountant's job to predict the future and say whether this firm is going to stick around or not. In cases where auditors are sued, the suit typically states that the auditor "knew or should have known." In this case the bank would argue that the auditor should have known about the problem. He cannot be expected to predict the future, but given all the evidence, he should have known bankruptcy was going to happen.

Therefore, given the clean opinion, Meadow Creek will probably get the loan and there is some chance that the firm may still go under. If a qualified opinion is given, however, Meadow Creek is not going to get the loan; as a result, 200 people will be out of a job.

Discussion

Stice:

That is a difficult consequence to accept. Two hundred people are going to be out of work. From an accounting perspective, what facts make a difference? What facts really matter? Does it matter that there are 200 people that are going to be out of a job?

Our concern is what we discovered during the course of an audit, from an accounting point of view and from a staff auditor point of view. We are concerned about the obsolete inventory, the contingencies, and the receivable question. Is this company a going concern? But, when it comes to stepping out of those auditor shoes and looking at this from an ethical perspective, does it matter that there are 200 people affected? Should that bias the decision at all?

Comment:

It is hard not to have feelings for those involved, but the rules do not address the issue of the effect of the auditor's opinion on the company.

Furthermore, the issue of being sued by the bank is not an issue at all. If you do the job that is supposed to be done, then that issue goes away. If you do not do the job that is supposed to be done, then the threat of a lawsuit exists; but then you have not done the job in the first place.

Stice:

I agree with that. Assuming we do the best we can, we could still possibly get sued. That is a terrible result but it is true. We can get sued even though we have done a picture-perfect audit. What can we do? Should we take the two extremes?

Comment:

When things were getting tight with litigation in a national firm, their policy involved writing an opinion on every section that was audited. Memos written by a brand new staff person required approval by everybody up the line, including the partner who signed off on the job. If he could not convince the staff person that his position was right and the staff person's was wrong, it went to the national audit. If something comes up later in litigation and the memo is not properly answered, the juror cannot be convinced that the staff person and the partner, both of whom disagreed on the issue, are both right.

Stice:

What are other options, aside from the extremes? Would it ever get so bad that you may say, "I just cannot play anymore?"

Comment:

First, as a young accountant, it is important to make those hard decisions before you are ever faced with the situation. When the case comes up, that decision is already made. When you have a mortgage and six kids, it is pretty tough to make the right choice, but if you make it now, it is not as hard.

Second, before you take action, make sure that you are right. What does the manager know that you may not know — a little more information, a little more experience? Consider SAS59, which deals specifically with going concerns. In SAS59 the standard says, evaluate whether there is a going concern problem or not. If there is, consult with management and see what they are going to do about it.

So, before you get upset and wonder what you are going to do for your next career, make sure you have all the information, because with a little experience you pick up a little expertise.

Stice:

What about the issue of underbilling to Universal? Did Universal do something illegal? Should you just tell Meadow Creek, "You have an invoice that has been issued in error." If you do, you have a violation of confidentiality that is almost inevitable. What should be done?

Comment:

If you make the receivable known to Meadow Creek, Universal will be disgruntled to say the least. But, consider your position at Universal when you audit them next time, now that you have seen their breach of ethics. That would make you wonder what else they were hiding on the audit.

You now have the option of not auditing them, which in fact is your obligation if you have a client whose performance you question and it cannot be resolved to your satisfaction. You have an obligation to withdraw from that assignment.

In fact, with publicly-traded companies you are required to file a report if they change auditors. Therefore, you could disclose the disagreement there. If you tell Universal that you are going to both withdraw from their engagement and tell everybody why, they might consider owning up to the receivable. This is a very possible solution for the auditors, with almost no risk involved.

Stice:

Unrelated to this case and not necessarily on an audit, but in general, what happens when the higher-ups pressure you? What if the overall attitude of the company is, "Let's cut those corners, let's make a buck, let's add as much to the bottom line as we can?" How do you fight that?

Some accountants and staff have been pressured by managers to charge overtime from an audit to the firm's general account rather than the client.

Then there is the related issue of the person who is over the budget, who does extra work and does not charge the client.

As a manager what would you think of a young accountant who did what you told him? Is that the way to get in with the boss, to do what they tell you? Or should you stand up for what you believe in and do what is right? What is the way to the top?

Comment:

There is a very practical answer to that issue, when somebody asks you as a young accountant to do some work and not charge the job. The answer lies in the fact that you might succeed to the management of that job and then what have you done? You've built yourself a hole, because your manager was able to present to his boss a job that was done in 100 hours, while an additional 40 hours were hidden somewhere else. Now, when you move up to the manager level and cannot do a job for that same 100 hours, you have built yourself a hole that you are not going to be able to get out of without being just as unethical.

The other problem is that you are perceived in the office to be a very high achiever. You can turn out an amazing amount of work in no time. You are tremendously efficient. All of a sudden you are completely inundated. There is the expectation that you can work that way. It is hard not to feel the pressure to continue and you just cannot keep it up. The best response, if asked by a manager not to charge time, is simply "I only have one way to be graded around here and that is my chargeability and the quality of the work I put out. I think it is only fair that if someone is going to pay the price that it ought to be you, who has some other way to keep your perception high in the firm."

Comment:

Another prevalent issue young accountants should remember is to watch what is going on and keep themselves above board at all times. There are little temptations that will come along. The first step is very easy or relatively easy — a very small step. But once you have taken that step, the path becomes better lighted and it is easier to take the next step and then the next.

Stice:

Consider Bill McKay's accountant. Bill McKay says, "I don't care what you think that inventory is worth, it is worth $100,000." What do you do? Later when it is found out, he says, "Well, ask my accountant, he is the one that is responsible for that."

Comment:

I recall a case in Washington. The accountant for a company was told by her two bosses, "You just pay the payroll, we will do the taxes." Later, the bosses mysteriously disappeared, and the IRS came to the woman and said, "What about those taxes?" The woman said, "Those guys told me they were taking care of it." And what did the IRS say? "Well, we know where you are, we don't know where they are. You owe us the money." And they got it. It was up to her to find the bosses and get the money.

Consequently, even though we may not be the boss, there are still potential problems as accountants, not CPAs, but young accountants in industry as well.

Stice:

It is tempting to say, "He is the manager and he must know more than I do." Eventually, however, you find out that he is doing it wrong. Are you responsible to alert the press?

Comment:

Companies get around this in part by having audit committees where you can bypass management. In this case, if there is a problem and nobody wants to do anything about it, you can go to one of Bill McKay's friends. Certainly they would like to know what is going on. And we have not even considered the obligation to shareholders. Don't the ten friends who are about to lose $450,000 have a right to know what Bill McKay is doing?

When it comes to young accountants, and our related ethical problems, one thing we can do is document it and send it up the levels in the firm. In most cases that is all we can do. We can make sure that we have all the information. Make sure that the manager does not have something that we do not know about before we fly off the handle. Also, find a partner/mentor who can help you in dilemmas like this. If you have a problem, you can go to them and they can give you a little advice.

In this case, we were also faced with the matter of judgment. Is it a violation of the rules or is it just a different interpretation? Is it just an honest disagreement in judgment or is it a fundamental violation of ethics? Finally, make your decisions early in life and set your own policy of ethics independent of the situation.

Questions

1. When making decisions, whose perspective should an accountant take, the firms, the client's, the users, or their own?
2. Why doesn't unethical behavior become easier after the first occurrence?
3. What part do audit committees play in easing the problems of unethical behavior?

____16
Why I Compromised My Professional Code of Ethics ____

McKINLEY L. TABOR

Mr. Tabor worked as the controller of the First National Bank of Crossville,
Tennessee. Earlier he worked for three years for Main, PMM & Company
as a staff accountant. He was formerly a Certified Public Accountant. He
presently works for an outdoor resort company helping with internal con-
trol.

Introduction ____

Not long ago the Institute of Financial Crime Prevention (now the
National Association of Certified Fraud Examiners) made a movie
about fraud and white collar crime. In that movie they featured the
stories of three people who have committed crimes. McKinley Tabor
is one of those people.

Mr. Tabor worked with Peat, Marwick, Mitchell as a CPA for
three years. He left and went to work for a bank, First National Bank
of Crossville Tennessee. After working there for some time, he became
their controller. While in the position of controller, he made a mistake
and took some money. He has since had to pay for his crime.

In this chapter, McKinley Tabor tells us why he breached his CPA
Code of Ethics and stole from his employer. He also shares with us
how his experience hurt him and how much suffering he has gone
through because of that mistake.

McKinley L. Tabor — Personal Background ____

I am the flip side of the coin to all of the other people that have
authored a chapter in this book about ethics. The flip side of my coin
is that I compromised my ethics. It is not something that I am proud
of; I am very much ashamed of it.

_____

Reprinted by permission of McKinley L. Tabor.

In searching for a way of demonstrating to you why I became unethical, an idea came to me not too long ago when my five year old daughter and I traveled back to my hometown to watch my 12-year-old son participate in his first band concert. On the way home after the concert, it was quiet, and my daughter crawled up in the seat beside me and went to sleep. I looked down at her and I felt that powerful surge, the swelling in my throat, for this little human being who was laying beside me. I thought, "I'm proud of her. And I'm proud of my 12-year-old." But that gave me the clue as to why I did what I did. In reality, the flip side of that pride in my children was misplaced pride in myself and my status.

Let me digress just a bit and tell you about McKinley Tabor. College educated beyond a Baccalaureate Degree, I have a Master of Banking degree from the Banking School at Louisiana State University — the first member of the Tabor clan, if you will, who completed his college education. I was the stereotype of "a big duck in a little pond" in my hometown community where my family was very prominent. In fact, my father was the highest elected official for the county; he carried the title of county judge, or county administrator. As a result, we were well known in the community. There was no one that didn't know me and my family, and there were very few people that I didn't know.

After completing my college education, I went to work for Peat, Marwick, Main and Co. Later, I moved back to my hometown and stepped into the local business. The largest local bank hired me (I think more for the prominence I had in the community than for my accounting expertise). I took that position and was very visible in the community. Soon after, I married a local girl and we both accustomed ourselves to the prominence and lifestyle of my position. I realize that this may all start sounding like a fairy tale, but let me tell you that it took a nasty turn.

While at the bank I entered into an investment partnership with the president of the bank and the head lending officer. In the banking industry, it is all too easy to get in over your head and I did. We borrowed sums of money from upstream correspondents (banks) and got into quite a few local businesses. In 1980, when interest rates went to 21 percent and the debt service was almost unbearable, I had significant financial pressures and did things that I should not have done. I compromised my professional code of ethics.

Reasons for Unethical Conduct

There are many reasons for ethical misconduct, but I have been able to pinpoint mine as misplaced pride. I was not able to accept the alternatives that were available to me at that time. For example, I could have declared bankruptcy. Alternatively, I could have entered into workout agreements with those lending institutions, or I could have gone to my family for help, but my own misplaced pride didn't allow me to accept any of those options.

I perceived my father to be more than just a father. To me, he was successful and respected in the community. My father was raised during the depression and he was devoutly opposed to mortgages, monthly payments, and borrowings in any way. Consequently, I was embarrassed to go to my family for help during this time of financial crisis. Bankruptcy was also totally ruled out because of who I was and what I did. It was just not a viable alternative for the vice president and chief financial officer of this community bank to file for bankruptcy. In addition, my position at the bank would have been jeopardized by trying to work out arrangements with these lending banks. So, instead of accepting the situation, towing the line, and doing what I should have done, I did something that I should not have done.

Results of Unethical Behavior

During that time I lost 95 pounds and all of my hair. The stresses involved were considerable. Naturally, those stresses were taken home with me at night, causing my first marriage to suffer, deteriorate, and finally die.

From that failed marriage, I bore additional guilt for leaving the two young sons I had at home. My solution was to create more financial burdens by trying to buy my children's love. So, in effect, I was maintaining two households and struggling to survive under some monumental debt service. All of these things came to bear on me. They are not any excuse for what I did, but they were extenuating circumstances.

My crime, in terms of dollars and cents, was not all that great. Primarily, I was not motivated by greed, and I certainly had no drug problem. Mine was a crime of taking what I should not have to maintain my current lifestyle. The crimes were fairly insignificant; they did not amount to any great amount of money but the consequences were life shattering. My life was turned completely upside down.

In the final analysis, I lost my CPA license. I lost 21 months out of my life. I'm still making restitution payments, and I've had to deal with the IRS for the taxes involved in my crime. My punishment, in my own mind, fits the crime, and I am not in any way bitter for what has happened to me. In fact, I rejoice somewhat because it has given me a new beginning. I have been able to pay for what I have done and with this new start I will be able to live under a code of ethics in both my personal and my professional life that is befitting what I do.

As for the future, I have been accepted by a new employer who recognizes the worth of someone who has done wrong and is dedicated to not doing wrong again. I have a new marriage that is very solid. My wife stood by me during the worst of times. I have a new little daughter who is the light of my life; and I am reestablishing my relationship with my two sons. So, there is life after punishment, but the price that I have had to pay for being unethical certainly makes the crime not worthwhile.

Discussion

Question:

Were you thinking, at the time, that you would reach a stage where you could repay those debts?

Tabor:

First, let me say that I worked for that bank for seven years, the first five of which were perfect years. The bank grew from being a $40 million bank to a $100 million bank. During that time I did absolutely nothing wrong. Later, when the financial pressures intensified from outside, I went through a time period where I fudged a little bit. I may have made a payment on my credit card and not immediately made that payment good from my personal funds. I may have waited until the end of the month.

My responsibilities in the bank were fairly broad. There was nothing that I did not do except lending. It was my responsibility to reconcile the bank's accounts. As a result, it was easy to fudge because only I was looking at what I was doing. There was a laxity of controls. My personal financial burdens, however, became so great that no longer did I fudge in that gray area, but I actually defrauded the bank of money. My thinking at the time was that I would always make it right. Unfortunately, it got to the point where I could not rectify my actions and still maintain the image of "McKinley Tabor" that was held by myself and the community.

Question:

Was this a one time affair or was there a sequence of events?

Tabor:

My crime involved 23 separate instances over a 26 month period. Once it was behind me and I got away with it the first time, the second time was all too easy. We did not have a good, strong internal auditor — in fact the auditor came to me for guidance. I never lied to the auditor; he simply never found anything that I did wrong. In addition, the bank at that time was having severe problems with their lending. As a result, the external auditors' and the FDIC auditors' focus was always on the lending area, never operations. Relatively speaking, I had no one looking over my shoulder. I answered directly to the board in most instances, and the board members were all good family friends by now.

Question:

What type of pressures caused you to commit this crime?

Tabor:

I don't think that I could convey to you totally all of the pressures that were going on with me. Primarily I had business, domestic, and physical problems that all came to a head, and I finally just threw my hands up and said, "I cannot deal with this any longer." I went into severe depression. I took a leave of absence from the bank, and I literally laid on a couch for a month. I pulled myself out of that position, left the bank, and went to another financial institution for employment. Subsequent to my leaving, however, one of the items, was discovered.

My responsibilities included managing the bank's bond portfolio. It amounted to about $48 million at the highest point. On one occasion, I sold a bond and received the accrued interest at the time of sale. But the brokerage house I sold it through made a mistake and sent me a check for the duplicate interest. I negotiated that duplicate check for my own benefit. Subsequent to my leaving the bank, that brokerage house discovered their error, applied to the bank for repayment of their duplicate payment, and that is when the house of cards fell. I immediately made restitution on it, entered into a restitution agreement with the bonding company, and I am still living up to that. I was caught because that duplicate payment was discovered. When they started looking, the bank spent a great deal more money on the investigation than the sum of money I actually took.

Question:

If the bank would have had stronger internal controls, might they have persuaded you not to take the money?

Tabor:

It would have dissuaded me more, but I feel that if somebody chooses to steal, they will steal. Weighing the risks against the benefits eventually results in a loss of focus until a person finally compromises, as I did.

Question:

You mentioned a total of 23 different incidences of improper transactions on your part. How did this come about? Were you looking for opportunities that were odd and diverse in the nature of the transactions or were they all of a similar type?

Tabor:

For the most part, all the transactions were similar. Often, I would get a telephone call telling me, "You have interest due, we need some money." I would simply issue a bank cashier's check or money order or traveler's check and follow it up later with a debit to a bank expense account. The bank was in an expanding mode at the time. We had a very large advertising budget and most of the items were under a normal audit scrutiny level. I was able to simply run a bank expense through the system without any kind of documentation to back it up.

Question:

What suggestions do you have on a personal basis, as well as on an institutional basis, to keep something like this from happening again?

Tabor:

On a personal basis I would suggest: know what your limits are and be in control. Be able to put in perspective the image you have of yourself. I could not. With my background, with the perception I had of myself in the community, with the pride that I had, I failed to do this. For your own best interest, be able to put pride behind you.

On a professional level, I view the situation from an accounting standpoint. The internal controls that were in place in the organization at that time were not sufficient to stop me or anyone else from being dishonest. In fact, being in charge of the teller line, I had to discipline people for the same misconduct that I was doing myself.

Now I am employed. I don't work in a national bank anymore, but I do still work in accounting and I design internal control systems for my employer. Now I look beyond the numbers that are on paper, I look at the people who are using those numbers. I try to find out what is behind them, what is going on in their personal lives, their outside business interests, and other clues that might help me prevent a breach of conduct.

Question:

As the bank's senior, what prevented you from putting controls into place when you were walking the straight line?

Tabor:

Again, the bank was in a rapid growth situation. An organization is handled differently in a $100 million bank as opposed to a $40 million bank. During that rapid growth period, there were other items that required attention aside from establishing the best internal controls. The bank also did not see fit to employ a real strong internal auditor who was autonomous from all others in the bank. In fact, both formally and informally, he came to me with questions and concerns. The bank had a lot of problems at this time because of its growth in lending. Their emphasis was on documentation and controls in the lending department, not in operations.

Question:

Describe your experience with criminal justice procedures. Did you plead guilty? What was prison like?

Tabor:

About 18 months passed from the time a U.S. marshall came knocking on my door to the time I pled guilty. I did not make the system go through an indictment process, but I did contest some of the 23 items. In some ways, I was unlucky because my trial occurred during the time of the Butchers in Tennessee. There was much adverse publicity pertaining to bankers and bank fraud at the time. Nonetheless, I was correctly punished for what I did. I harbor no bitter feelings. The 21 months that I spent incarcerated gave me time to reflect and to get a good grip on myself, if you will. I lost much during that period, such as time with my family. In jail, I was subjected to circumstances unlike anything I had ever known. Incidently, some would say I was in a country club — I didn't serve hard time.

As soon as I got in jail and people found out who I was and what I knew, I was given the job of a clerk in the dormitory in which I resided. I immediately took control of where the inmates slept and where they worked. Later, the warden decided that the clerks had a little bit too much authority and he abolished that position.

From there, I went to work in the prison industries in a factory doing almost the same work that I had done out on the street. I was an accountant in a cut and sew textile factory, ordering materials and scheduling job orders, for the remainder of my prison term. I made more money than anybody else in jail except for the people who worked at the factory. This was not hard time, but it was a good time to reflect. I went to work at 7:00 in the morning and finished at 4:00 in the afternoon. So, to answer the question, I was punished in more ways than just time taken out of my life, but I am a better person for the experience.

Question:

You mentioned the desire you had to build an image in your early career. Would you describe your feelings now on needing to have a similar image?

Tabor:

I have no need whatsoever to rebuild the previous image that I had of myself. I was determined to own "things," to make a lot of money, and to be the "big duck in the little pond." Now I focus on my children, my family life, and experiences instead of "things." I like to go places and meet new people, where before I liked to own cars and have big bank accounts. These experiences last much longer than a dollar bill.

Questions

1. What caused Mr. Tabor to compromise his ethics? Were each of the necessary points (i.e. rationalization, opportunity, and pressure) involved?
2. Where could Mr. Tabor have stopped the downturn in his behavior? Could he have eliminated the problem if he had thought about unethical behavior early in his career? How early should he have dealt with these concerns?
3. What makes Mr. Tabor different from other people in the same situation?
4. How was pride involved in his crime? Is this usually the case?

Epilogue
Reflection of the Issues
Raised In This Book _____

DR. KEVIN D. STOCKS

Dr. Stocks received his doctoral degree in Accounting from Oklahoma State University. He is currently an Associate Professor in the School of Accountancy at Brigham Young University. Dr. Stocks' areas of specialization include cost/managerial accounting and information systems. He is a member of the AAA, the AICPA, and the NAA.

In an effort to summarize the ideas conveyed in this book, I will rely on the thought that if you get one good idea, your time reading was well spent. With that in mind, let me suggest nine good ideas that I have gathered from this pool of ethical issues.

A basic question discussed in this text is whether ethics is a new issue. The suggested response is that ethics is not new; however, the point is that ethics is a real issue, a very current issue, and it is one that needs to be addressed. Simply the awareness of ethics as an important issue is a valuable point.

What causes unethical behavior? The answer to this question can be viewed in a number of ways. Steve Albrecht mentioned that pressure, opportunity, and rationalization are ways to view the problem of unethical behavior. Also, self-deception, self-indulgence, self-protection, and self-righteousness support other views. The point is that unethical behavior is common and reasons exist for such behavior. We need to examine and understand those reasons. Once we have an understanding of the reasons for unethical behavior, we can then look at what can be done to combat the problem.

We must ask ourselves, "What is needed?" One response to this question centers on the need for a fundamental principle of goodness. Recently, I attended a presentation by a child psychologist who spoke on how to raise moral children. It was a fascinating presentation and very much on the same topic of ethical behavior. He put into usable terms the concept of a fundamental principle of goodness.

Reprinted by permission of Dr. Kevin D. Stocks.

The child psychologist said that morality must be explained to children on a level that they can understand. His definition of morality was an intent or action to help another person or persons. This leaves, then, the definition of immorality as the intent or action to hurt another person or persons. Children understand "help" and they understand "hurt" and they can work with these concepts. As we get a little older and into more complex situations, the details get slightly more difficult and sometimes trade-offs exist, but ethical behavior really boils down to helping versus hurting others.

As accountants we must recognize that our ethical behavior is not simply bound by what we view as ethical but what is viewed as ethical by those watching us. As was illustrated in an earlier chapter, if your children were watching you, even the implication that there might be some ethical problems in what you are doing would be important enough for you to re-examine your behavior. This is an issue that greatly affects accountants.

The issue of ethical versus legal should be considered in greater depth. As previously mentioned, legality is the lowest denominator of acceptable ethical behavior. My personal hope is that the limit of legality is never approached in most of my ethical considerations.

Ethics applies to everything, everywhere, always. One of the questions addressed in the Management Accountant case was, "Does the management accountant, as a professional, park his or her personal ethics at the door when going into the company?" Let me suggest that you should not park your ethics at the door at any time. You do not park it when you go home. You do not park it when you go to church. You do not park it when you go to school. And, you certainly do not park it when you go to the office. The idea that "this is business and therefore dishonesty is okay," or "this is school and therefore cheating is okay," is wrong. Ethics applies at all times, in all places, and in all situations.

We have addressed the question, "Good ethics is equal to what?" Ideally, good ethics is equal to good business; however, good ethics does not equal winning every time. The difference between good business and winning every time is the fact that good business is a long-term orientation. Good ethics equals good business over the long run. Too often we have the misperception that good ethics equals winning, profit making, and obtaining the desired consequence in every situation.

One chapter focused on the development process of morality and ethics. Perhaps ethics can be taught during the college experience. The idea is that between the ages of 20 and 30, as individuals leave the nest and head out into the world and establish their own business patterns, they really learn and establish their ethical standards for the future. While I believe that this statement is true, I also believe that we are all developing, nurturing, and establishing our ethical standards and behaviors at all points of our lives. With the recognition of continual development, discussion on the topic of ethics becomes more and more important.

Whose responsibility is it to teach ethical behavior? Who has the responsibility to monitor behavior? Because the only person you have any control over is yourself, the responsibility must start from within. We must all ensure that our own behavior is ethical, our business choices are ethical and appropriate, and that our interaction with others takes place in an ethical manner. As we make ethics the foundation of our own activities, we will begin to have greater opportunities to build and influence the ethical foundations of others.

Quotes on Ethics in Accounting and Business

No institution, be it General Motors, the federal government, or Brigham Young University, can fill its rightful place in the scheme of things unless there is a strong moral and ethical base undergirding its operations and overarching its philosophy.

—President Gordon B. Hinckley
First Presidency of The Church of Jesus Christ of Latter-day Saints

I have but one system of ethics for men and for nations—to be grateful, to be faithful in all engagements and under all circumstances, to be open and generous, promoting in the long run even the interests of both.

—Thomas Jefferson

One thing that concerns me about the future of our country is the preoccupation with profits we see in the financial area, as opposed to concern for people and values. One of the reasons for our competitive malaise may be that we have lost sight of what organizations are supposed to do.

—John J. Mackowski
Chairman and CEO, Atlantic Mutual Companies

I never met a corporation with a conscience.

—George Meany

Among the board of directors of Fortune 500 companies I estimate that 95 percent are not fully doing what they are legally, morally and ethically supposed to do.

—Harold Green, former CEO, ITT

That's the American way. If little kids don't aspire to make money like I did, what the hell good is this country?

—Lee Iacocca (*Newsweek*, May 11, 1987)

Greed in business is all right. Greed's healthy. You can be greedy and still feel good about yourself.

—Ivan Boesky, at Berkeley's Business School graduation exercise

Willy Loman: *"To suffer fifty weeks of the year for the sake of a two-week vacation, when all you really desire is to be outside with your shirt off. And always to have to get ahead of the next fella. And still that's how you build a future.*
—Arthur Miller, *Death of a Salesman*

For the Confucian—but also for the philosopher of the Western tradition—only law can handle the rights and objections of collectives. Ethics is always a matter of the person.
—Peter Drucker

Be ye lamps unto yourselves; be your own reliance. Hold to the truth within yourselves as to the only lamp.
—Buddha

The pursuit of wealth and power is so pervasive today as to create something that may be entirely new—namely, a money culture. When such a culture goes cheek-by-jowl with extreme poverty, it is potentially dangerous.
—Felix G. Rohatyn
Senior Partner, Lazard Freres & Company

We need to dangle two or three people by their thumbs in the rotunda on the Capitol as an example of what we do to wrongdoers in the West.
—Former Utah Governor Scott M. Matheson
commenting on Utah stock frauds

More than 100 members of the Reagan Administration have had ethical or legal charges leveled against them. That number is without precedent. While the Reagan Administration's missteps may not have been as flagrant as the Teapot Dome scandal or as pernicious as Watergate, they seem more general, more pervasive and somehow more ingrained than those of any previous administration.
—*Time* article, "Morality Among the Supplysiders"

Being ethical requires that you be committed, especially when it is not convenient, popular, or lucrative to do so.
—Kenneth H. Blanchard
Chairman, Blanchard Training and Development

Senior management plays the most important role in producing ethical behavior. Senior management, beginning with the CEO, creates the ethical tone of the corporation by setting standards and living up to them. The rest of the organization will follow their example. Setting a good example is not enough, however. The CEO must also ensure clear, consistent communication of the corporation's values to all employees. A key part of that communication must be that unethical practices will simply not be tolerated.

—William D. Smithburg
  Chairman and CEO, The Quaker Oats Company

Millions of Americans desperately search for a moral rock upon which to stand in what feels like a swamp of values.

—Eric Sevareid, Senior Consultant, CBS

Moral times of a nation is established by its professional people.

—Judge Lloyd George

America is great because she is good, and if America ever ceases to be good, America will cease to be great.

—Alex de Tocqueville

A man of integrity will never listen to a plea against his conscience.

—Oliver Wendell Holmes

Make yourself an honest man, and then you may be sure there is one rascal less in the world.

—Carlyle

Business ethics are not different from personal ethics.

—Russell E. Palmer, Dean, The Wharton School

Ethics must begin with one's individual commitment to doing what is right.

—Edward A. Kangas, Touche Ross

It is imperative that those who serve the public interest be held to higher standards of ethics, morality, and accountability than any others.

—John G. Tower, former U.S. Senator, (R-TX)

Business must work to build awareness that deal-making for fast bucks is wrong-headed and dangerous.

—Edward L. Hennessy, Jr., Chairman of Allied-Signal Inc.

Ethics is a moral compass. Ideally, it should coincide with enlightened self-interest, not only to avoid jail in the short run but to avoid social

upheaval in the long run. It must be embedded early, at home, in grade school, in church. It is highly personal. I doubt it can be taught in college.
—Felix G. Rohatyn, Senior Partner, Lazard Freres & Company

There is no right way to do a wrong thing.
—Kenneth H. Blanchard
    Chairman, Blanchard Training and Development

True education does not consist of merely acquiring of a few facts of science, history, literature, or art, but in the development of character.
—David O. McKay

All things whatsoever ye would that men should do to you, do ye even so to them.
—Bible, Matt. 7:12

To thine own self be true, and it must follow, as the night the day, thou canst not then be false to any man.
—William Shakespeare

A recent poll indicates that only a third of Americans believe business does a pretty good or better job of behaving ethically, and 53 percent believe most corporate executives are dishonest.
—*New York Times*

Ethical issues come down to the fundamental question of how much of today's benefit you are willing to forgo for tomorrow's gain.
—John H. Stookey
    President and Chairman, Quantum Chemical Corporation

It is remarkable how willing American business people are to make the current quarter look better at the expense of the future, to sacrifice the future to make this year's bottom line a little more attractive or less embarrassing.
—John Nasibitt, *Megatrends*

An overly ambitious employee might have the mistaken idea that we do not care how results are obtained, as long as he gets results. He might think it best not to tell higher management all that he is doing, not to record all transactions accurately ... He would be wrong on all counts ... We don't want liars for managers.
—Clifton C. Garvin, Jrs., Chairman of Exxon Corp.

Men are unqualified for civil liberty, in exact proportion to their disposition to put moral chains upon their own appetites; in proportion as their love for justice is above their capacity; in proportion as their soundness and sobriety of understanding is above their vanity and presumption; in proportion as they are more disposed to listen to the counsels of the wise and good, in preference to the flattery of knaves. Society cannot exist unless a controlling power upon will and appetite be placed somewhere, and the less of it there is within, the more there must be without. It is ordained in the eternal constitution of things, that men of intemperate minds cannot be free. Their passions forge their fetters.
—Sir Edmund Burke

So much then for people who fulfill their moral obligations sufficiently well to be regarded as good. But those who habitually weight the right course against what they regard as advantageous are in quite a different category. Unlike good men, they judge everything by profits and gains, which seem to them just as valuable as what is right ... For preferring advantage to right is not the only crime. It is also sinful even to attempt a comparison between the two things—even to hesitate between them.
—Cicero, "On Duties"

Never value the advantages derived from anything involving breach of faith, loss of self-respect, hatred, suspicion, or execration of others, insincerity, or the desire for something which has to be veiled and curtained.
—Marcus Aurelius, *Megatrends*

—*Industry Week* survey comments from respondents included:

My observations suggest that the more successful the businessman, the more unethical the behavior.

We have a policy regarding ethics, but middle management ignores the rules by rationalizing, `that's not unethical, it's just smart business.'

Ethics is fast losing the battle; profit is number one at any expense.

Anything goes; our policy is if you can get away with it, do it.

There are no ethics any more; use whatever works for profit.

Business students come to us from our society. If they haven't been taught ethics by their families, their clergymen, their elementary and secondary schools, their liberal arts colleges or engineering school or the business firms where most of them have already worked prior to getting a business degree, there is very little we can do.

Ethics will be restored when most individuals come to the realization that they play for a common team and are willing to sacrifice self-interest for the team.

The question 'Is it right?' is not the same as 'Is it legal?' Yet most Americans act as if it were so.

—Lester C. Thurow, Dean, Sloan School of Management, MIT

We must replace the ethic of efficient trading with an approach that emphasizes productive building.

—Edward L. Hennessy
  Mr., Chairman, and CEO, Allied-Signal Inc.

The sad truth is becoming more and more apparent. Our profession has seen a steady decline by casting aside established traditions and canons of professional ethics that evolved over the centuries.

—Former Chief Justice Warren E. Burger

All across our country, there is evidence of a deterioration of ethics. Nowhere is this decline greater than in the world of business. Honest, caring, rational individuals seemingly have come to check their values at the door when they enter the office. The attitude in many businesses appears to be profit at any cost, especially if a company's gains can be at the expense of a competitor—and, sometimes even if it is at the expense of its customers.

—Kenneth H. Blanchard
  Chairman, Blanchard Training and Development

The challenge for management is to create the algorithms, the check-lists ... and the systems which will put the spotlight on the ethicality of its decision.

—Alden G. Lank
  Director of Studies, International Management Institute, Geneva, Switzerland

In the end, business ethics is merely a reflection of American ethics.

—Lester C. Thurow, Dean, Sloan School of Management, MIT

If you tell your managers, 'You've got to reach this number' time and time again, they're going to focus on reaching that number and not on how they reach it. And that behavior is reinforced when individuals are promoted who have ignored the 'how' and have cut ethical corners to meet the quarterly profit and performance objectives.

—Patricia Rainey Reese
  Director, Finance and Administration, The Ethics Resource Center

_____Bibliography_____

A truly good book teaches me better than to read it. I must soon lay it down and commence living on its hints . . . What I began by reading, I must finish by acting.

— Henry Thoreau

BOOKS

1. *Ethics in American Business: A Special Report* by Touche Ross Co., 1988.
2. *Ethics in American Business: An Opinion Survey of Key Business Leaders on Ethical Standards and Behavior* by Touche Ross, Co., 1988.
3. *Papers on the Ethics of Administration* edited by N. Dale Wright, Brigham Young University, 1988.
4. *Moral Problems in Contemporary Society: Essays in Humanistic Ethics* edited by Paul Kurtz, Prentice-Hall Inc., © 1969.
5. *The Conscience of the Corporations* by Jules Cohn, The Johns Hopkins Press, © 1971.
6. *Nicomachean Ethics* by Aristotle, translated by Terence Irwin, Hackett Publishing Company, © 1985.
7. *Management and Machiavelli* by Antony Jay, Holt, Rinehart and Winston, © 1967.
8. *The Power of Ethical Management* by Kenneth H. Blanchard and Norman Vincent Peale, (Morrow-New York), 1988.
9. *Corporate Strategy and the Search for Ethics* by R. Edward Freeman and Daniel R. Gilbert, Jr. (Prentice-Hall), 1988.
10. *Ethics in the Marketplace,* John Casey, 1988.
11. *Ethics and Morals in Business* by Samuel M. Natale, Birmingham, Alabama: REP, 1983.
12. *Policies and Persons: A Casebook in Business Ethics* by John B. Matthews, Kenneth E. Goodpaster, and Laura L. Nash, New York: McGraw-Hill Book Company, 1985.
13. *A Bibliography of Business Ethics 1976-1980* by Donald G. Jones and Helen Troy, Charlottesville: University Press of Virginia, 1982.
14. *Ethics in the Business Curriculum: A Preliminary Survey of Undergraduate Business Programs* by George L. Pamental, New York: University Press of America, 1988.

ARTICLES

1. "The Decline and Fall of Business Ethics" by Myron Magnet, *Fortune* (December 8, 1986).
2. "The Inseparability of Economics and Morality," The American Economic Foundation.
3. "Morality Test: Special Report on Ethics," *U.S. News and World Report* (December 9, 1985).
4. "Cleaning Up Wall Street," *Insight* (March 23, 1987).
5. "Organizational Statesmanship and Dirty Politics: Ethical Guidelines for the Organizational Politician," *Organizational Dynamics* (Autumn 1983).
6. "Christian Values and the Corporation" by Hicks B. Waldron, Chairman and Chief Executive Officer, Avon Products, Inc. (May 6, 1985).
7. "Ethics in America's Money Culture" by Felix G. Rohatyn, *New York Times* (Wed., June 3, 1987).
8. "Ethical Chic" by Peter F. Drucker, *Forbes* (September 14, 1981).
9. "The Ethical Side of Enterprise" by Verne E. Henderson, *Sloan Management Review* (Spring 1982).
10. "Is the Ethics of Business Changing?" by Steven N. Brenner and Earl A. Molander, *Harvard Business Review* (January-February 1977).
11. "The Rise and Fall of an Insider" by Steven Brill, *The American Lawyer*, © 1986.
12. "Performance Lies are Hazardous to Organizational Health" by Lee T. Perry and Jay B. Barney, *Organizational Dynamics* (Winter 1981).
13. "Blowing the Whistle on Corporate Misconduct" by D. Clutterbuck, *International Management* (January 1980).
14. "Business Ethics: A Manager's Primer" by Gene Laczniak, *Business* (January-March, 1983).
15. "Whistleblowing" by Myron Peretz Glazer and Penina Migdal Glazer, *Psychology Today*, © 1986.
16. "A Question of Ethics" by J.B. Ritchie and Thomas W. Dunfee, *Wall Street Journal: The College Edition of the National Business Employment Weekly* (Spring 1987).
17. "The Challenge of Professional and Public Service Ethics for Latter-day Saints" by Gordon B. Hinckley, February 19, 1988.
18. "Ethics and Internal Auditors," *The Internal Auditor* (April 1989).
19. "The Concentric Circles of Management Thought" by William G. Scott.

*20. "Character Ethics and Organizational Life" by David L.
Norton.
"The Sympathetic Organization" by David K. Hart.
"The Paradox of Profit" by Norman E. Bowie.
"Ethics and Responsibility" by Kenneth D. Walters.
"The Motivating Power of Ethics in Times of Corporate
Confusion" by Margaret J. Wheatley.
"Organizational Ethics: Paradox and Paradigm" by J. Bonner
Ritchie.
"Reason of State as Political Morality: A Benign View" by
John A. Rohr.
"Ethical Theory and Public Service" by F. Neil Brady.

*All from *Papers on the Ethics of Administration*, edited by N. Dale Wright, Brigham
Young University Press, © 1988.

APPENDIX

The Professional Code of Ethics

Principles of Professional Conduct

Preamble

.01 Membership in the American Institute of Certified Public Accountants is voluntary. By accepting membership, a certified public accountant assumes an obligation of self-discipline above and beyond the requirements of laws and regulations.

.02 These Principles of the Code of Professional Conduct of the American Institute of Certified Public Accounts express the profession's recognition of its responsibilities to the public, to clients, and to colleagues. They guide members in the performance of their professional responsibilities and express the basic tenets of ethical and professional conduct. The Principles call for an unswerving commitment to honorable behavior, even at the sacrifice of personal advantage.

Article I — Responsibilities

In carrying out their responsibilities as professionals, members should exercise sensitive professional and moral judgements in all their activities.

.01 As professionals, certified public accounts perform an essential role in society. Consistent with that role, members of the American

---

AICPA adapted.

Institute of Certified Public Accounts have responsibilities to all those who use their professional services. Members also have a continuing responsibility to cooperate with each other to improve the art of accounting, maintain the public's confidence, and carry out the profession's special responsibilities for self-governance. The collective efforts of all members are required to maintain and enhance the traditions of the profession.

Article II — The Public Interest

Members should accept the obligation to act in a way that will serve the public interest, honor the public trust, and demonstrate commitment to professionalism.

.01   A distinguishing mark of a profession is acceptance of its responsibility to the public. The accounting profession's public consists of clients, credit grantors, governments, employers, investors, the business and financial community, and others who rely on the objectivity and integrity of certified public accountants to maintain the orderly functioning of commerce. This reliance imposes a public interest responsibility on certified public accountants. The public interest is defined as the collective well-being of the community of people and institutions the profession serves.

.02   In discharging their professional responsibilities, members may encounter conflicting pressures from among each of those groups. In resolving those conflicts, members should act with integrity, guided by the precept that when members fulfill their responsibility to the public, clients' and employers' interests are best served.

.03   Those who rely on certified public accountants expect them to discharge their responsibilities with integrity, objectivity, due professional care, and a genuine interest in serving the public. They are expected to provide quality services, enter into fee arrangements, and offer a range of services — all in a manner that demonstrates a level of professionalism consistent with these Principles of the Code of Professional Conduct.

.04   All who accept membership in the American Institute of Certified Public Accountants commit themselves to honor the public trust. In return for the faith that the public reposes in them, members should seek continually to demonstrate their dedication to professional excellence.

Article III — Integrity

To maintain and broaden public confidence, members should perform all professional responsibilities with the highest sense of integrity.

.01   Integrity is an element of character fundamental to professional recognition. It is the quality from which the public trust derives and the benchmark against which a member must ultimately test all decisions.

.02   Integrity requires a member to be, among other things, honest and candid within the constraints of client confidentiality. Service and the public trust should not be subordinated to personal gain and advantage. Integrity can accommodate the inadvertent error and the honest difference of opinion; it cannot accommodate deceit or subordination of principle.

.03   Integrity is measured in terms of what is right and just. In the absence of specific rules, standards, or guidance, or in the face of conflicting opinions, a member should test decisions and deeds by asking: "Am I doing what a person of integrity would do? Have I retained my integrity?" Integrity requires a member to observe both the form and the spirit of technical and ethical standards; circumvention of those standards constitutes subordination of judgement.

.04   Integrity also requires a member to observe the principles of objectivity and independence and of due care.

Article IV — Objectivity and Independence _____

A member should maintain objectivity and be free of conflicts of interest in discharging professional responsibilities. A member in public practice should be independent in fact and appearance when providing auditing and other attestation services.

.01   Objectivity is a state of mind, a quality that lends value to a member's services. It is a distinguishing feature of the profession. The principle of objectivity imposes the obligation to be impartial, intellectually honest, and free of conflicts of interest. Independence precludes relationships that may appear to impair a member's objectivity in rendering attestation services.

.02   Members often serve multiple interests in many different capacities and must demonstrate their objectivity in varying circumstances. Members in public practice render attest, tax, and management advisory services. Other members prepare financial statements in the employment of others, perform internal auditing services, and serve in financial and management capacities in industry, education, and government. They also educate and train those who aspire to admission into the profession. Regardless of service or capacity, members should protect the integrity of their work, maintain objectivity, and avoid any subordination of their judgement.

.03   For a member in public practice, the maintenance of objectivity and independence requires a continuing assessment of client relationships and public responsibility. Such a member who provides auditing and other attestation services should be independent in fact and appearance. In providing all other services, a member should maintain objectivity and avoid conflicts of interest.

.04   Although members not in public practice cannot maintain the appearance of independence, they nevertheless have the responsibility to maintain objectivity in rendering professional services. Members employed by others to prepare financial statements or to perform auditing, tax, or consulting services are charged with the same responsibility for objectivity as members in public practice and must be scrupulous in their application of generally accepted accounting principles and candid in their dealings with members in public practice.

Article V — Due Care

A member should observe the profession's technical and ethical standards, strive continually to improve competence and the quality of services, and discharge professional responsibility to the best of the member's ability.

.01   The quest for excellence is the essence of due care. Due care requires a member to discharge professional responsibilities with competence and diligence. It imposes the obligation to perform professional services to the best of a member's ability with concern for the best interest of those for whom the services are performed and consistent with the profession's responsibility to the public.

.02   Competence is derived from a synthesis of education and experience. It begins with a mastery of the common body of knowledge required for designation as a certified public accountant. The maintenance of competence requires a commitment to learning and professional improvement that must continue throughout a member's professional life. It is a member's individual responsibility. In the engagements and in all responsibilities, each member should undertake to achieve a level of competence that will assure that the quality of the member's services meets the high level of professionalism required by the Principles.

.03   Competence represents the attainment and maintenance of a level of understanding and knowledge that enables a member to render services with facility and acumen. It also establishes the limitations of a member's capabilities by dictating that consultation or referral may be required when a professional engagement exceeds the personal competence of a member or a member's firm. Each member is responsible for assessing his or her own competence — of evaluating whether education, experience, and judgement are adequate for the responsibility to be assumed.

.04   Members should be diligent in discharging responsibilities to clients, employers, and the public. Diligence imposes the responsibility to render services promptly and carefully, to be thorough, and to observe applicable technical and ethical standards.

.05   Due care requires a member to plan and supervise adequately any professional activity for which he or she is responsible.

Article VI — Scope and Nature of Services _____

A member in public practice should observe the Principles of the Code of Professional Conduct in determining the scope and nature of services to be provided.

.01   The public interest aspect of certified public accountants' services requires that such services be consistent with acceptable professional behavior for certified public accountants. Integrity requires that services and the public trust not be subordinated to personal gain and advantage. Objectivity and independence require that members be free from conflicts of interest in discharging professional responsibilities. Due care requires that services be provided with competence and diligence.

.02   Each of these Principles should be considered by members in determining whether or not to provide specific services in individual circumstances. In some instances, they may represent an overall constraint on the nonaudit services that might be offered to a specific client. No hard-and-fast rules can be developed to help members reach these judgements, but they must be satisfied that they are meeting the spirit of the Principles in this regard.

.03   In order to accomplish this, members should

- Practice in firms that have in place internal quality-control procedures to ensure that services are competently delivered and adequately supervised.

- Determine, in their individual judgements, whether the scope and nature of other services provided to an audit client would create a conflict of interest in the performance of the audit function for that client.

- Assess, in their individual judgements, whether an activity is consistent with their role as professionals (for example, Is such activity a reasonable extension or variation of existing services offered by the member or others in the profession?).